It Runs in the Family

It Runs in the Family

UNDERSTANDING MORE ABOUT YOUR ANCESTORS

RUTH A. SYMES

The
History
Press

For Billy, Ruby and Robertson,
heralds of a new generation.

Cover Illustrations: *Front, clockwise from top*: author's collection; author's collection; author's collection; Gilesgate Archives and Beamish, The Living Museum of the North; *The Girl's Own Paper*, Mary and Sandra Jeffrey; public domain; author's collection; author's collection. *Back: The Girl's Own Paper, Home Words for Heart and Heart.*

First published 2013

The History Press
The Mill, Brimscombe Port
Stroud, Gloucestershire, GL5 2QG
www.thehistorypress.co.uk

© Ruth A. Symes, 2013

The right of Ruth A. Symes, to be identified as the Author
of this work has been asserted in accordance with the
Copyright, Designs and Patents Act 1988.

British Library Cataloguing in Publication Data.
A catalogue record for this book is available from the British Library.

ISBN 978 0 7524 9702 0

Typesetting and origination by The History Press
Printed in Great Britain

Contents

Introduction

AN INTIMATE GUIDE TO OUR ANCESTORS AND THEIR TIMES

How often have we all returned to old photographs, written records and objects that we have inherited from our ancestors, hoping that simply by doing so they will somehow magically throw up more of their secrets? But historical ephemera can be frustratingly unforthcoming if we are not sure how to 'read' them. More often than not we may close the photograph album, return the document to its envelope, or put the object back on its shelf with a sense of dissatisfaction. Our ancestor remains clouded in mystery – a person unknown. This book aims to show you new ways of looking at your family history material in order that you may better understand the times (or, more correctly, the culture) in which the photograph was taken, the record made or the object used, and through this process allow your ancestor finally to step out of the shadows and make him or herself better known to you.

Everything from the past – from a collar stud to a whiff of perfume – is a product of its era and can be interpreted as such. How your ancestor chose to show his cufflinks, design his tattoo or even shape her eyebrows has a great deal to do with the prevailing norms and beliefs of the period in which he or she was living. In this way of looking at things, a hairstyle in an old photograph is not just a matter of personal grooming but might indicate all sorts of information about your ancestor, from age and health to social class, and even position in the family. Likewise, how your ancestor wore his beard may lead you to speculate on his religious or military associations, as well as his manliness or personal attractiveness. And the story behind your ancestor's wedding ring might reveal something of her class status, her religious background, her income level and even her employment status – as well as, more obviously, her romantic life.

This book focuses mainly on the period from the beginning of the nineteenth century to the 1950s. During this time photographic records first became available to the general public, more official documentation was collected on ordinary people than ever before and mass consumerism meant that families owned many more material objects than they had done in earlier centuries. In the Victorian and Edwardian periods, and later in the twentieth century, many people visited photographic studios, created photo albums and came to own cameras of their own. The state also played its part in recording the more personal and intimate aspects of our ancestors' lives, through ten-yearly censuses, prison records, transportation records, military records and hospital records, to name but a few. Many of these records have now been made available to the family historian through the wonders of easily (and often freely) searchable Internet databases. Many, many more fascinating documents, including newspapers, diaries, letters and wills, lie in archives dotted around the country waiting to be examined. And there are other more tangible personal items: locks of hair, half-used bottles of aftershave, pressed flowers, and buttons and brooches, stashed away in attics and garages, lodged between the pages of old books and nestled in family jewellery boxes – all of which may tell their own tale.

Social historians have written about all the aspects of ordinary life that interest people researching their families in the past, from the state of the nation's teeth, diet, height and weight, to the ins and outs of the practice of shaving, the legal and economic connotations of wearing a wedding ring, and even the business of keeping a dog. One of the aims of this book is to make some of this research (including fascinating examples from magazines, poetry, novels and documentary studies of the past) accessible to the ordinary reader. Imagine history itself as a thick lock of hair: at whatever point you cut through it there will be multiple strands that make up that particular moment. This book looks at some of these strands: the superstitions and scientific beliefs, the fashions and medical advice, the developing manufacturing processes, penal laws, the situation of women and the condition of the working class, all of which characterised British society in the not-so-distant past. It will describe the role of empire, the horrors and deprivations of the two world wars, the development of criminal anthropology, the rise of national sovereignty and the cult of celebrity. And on the domestic front it will touch upon new ideas about weight, diet, personal cleanliness, correct behaviour and even sexuality that might have impacted on our ancestors' experiences. In short, this book touches on many of the threads that made society what it was at any given moment in the past. In glimpsing some of these, it is hoped that you will come to understand more about your ancestors as products of their times – and through that will come to understand them better as individuals as well.

Family history is not just an academic exercise, of course, and this book will include such practical genealogical matters as how to find out where and when ancestors who worked in particular professions (such as dentists) practised, and advice on making educated guesses about inherited belongings – why your ancestor might have chosen a particular stone in her engagement ring, for example. The 'Find Out More' sections at the end of each chapter will point to ways in which you can extend your knowledge and understanding of a particular topic through other books and websites. Of course, these resources are just the tip of the iceberg. The recent information revolution has made an almost infinite number of sources on any given subject available in our own homes at the touch of a button. Starting with the small matters of physical characteristics and personal effects, this book will give you strategies for sifting through some of this information and picking out what might be relevant to your family story.

There are a number of things that this book doesn't do. It does not, for example, offer scientific explanations on how physical characteristics might have been inherited; simple explanations of genetics are available on the Internet. Secondly, it does not offer a comprehensive history of photography, or an analysis of aspects of dress (or the other large props and backdrops) often visible in old photographs. These are topics much more ably addressed by my fellow family historians Jayne Shrimpton and Robert Pols. A list of some of their books on those subjects follows.

In family photographs from the past our ancestors stare out at us, somehow imploring us to understand them. The personal and official documents that record their lives likewise beg to be examined time and time again, and we have all turned over and over in our hands the objects that they used regularly, as if just by doing so we might come to know the people of the past better. This book should act as a magnifying glass turned on to that evidence, giving more prominence to these small matters. It should also act as a reading lamp, throwing light into the shadows and allowing you finally to get close to your ancestors in ways that you might never have believed possible.

FIND OUT MORE

Jayne Shrimpton, *British Working Dress*, Shire, 2012.

Jayne Shrimpton, *Family Photographs and How to Date Them*, Countryside Books, 2008.

Jayne Shrimpton, *How to Get the Most from Family Photographs*, Society of Genealogists Enterprises Ltd, 2011.

Robert Pols, *Dating Old Photographs*, second edition, FFHS Publications, 1998.

Robert Pols, *Understanding Old Photographs*, Robert Boyd Publications, 1995.

www.nationalarchives.gov.uk – the National Archives.

www.ancestry.co.uk; www.findmypast.co.uk; www.thegeneaologist.co.uk – online commercial websites dedicated to making available many genealogical databases.

Caught by the Lens

EYES

*L*ike all family historians you will, no doubt, have spent a great deal of time scrutinising the eyes of the men, women and children in family photographs or – in some more exalted cases – painted family portraits. While all the other features of an ancestor's image might give us clues to the material ways in which he or she lived, it is only in the eyes that something of his or her spirit is reflected.

The eyes in some portraits and photographs have that uncanny ability of following us around the room. This is a bizarre effect of any picture in which the subject is looking straight out of the canvas or straight at the lens, but it is a particularly unnerving one when the subject is an ancestor: we cannot but feel that they are casting a disapproving eye down the generations at us! The effect occurs because portraits and photographs are in two dimensions. The light, shadow and perspective depicted in each medium are fixed, and therefore don't shift as the viewer moves around the room. Thus the eyes look pretty much the same regardless of the angle from which you are looking at them – something that doesn't happen in (three-dimensional) real life.

Inevitably we consider the eyes of our ancestors looking for likenesses, for the shadows of generations not yet born. The shape of an ancestor's eyes might remind us of his or her ethnic background, but it is impossible to determine eye colour from sepia or black-and-white photographs. Some Victorian photos were hand coloured by artists, but in these cases it is highly unlikely that the artist would ever have met the sitter. He would simply have been given instructions to paint the eyes 'blue', 'green' or 'brown',

An unknown family in a Llandudno photographic studio, 1890s. The poses are typical: the father looks straight ahead with a confident gaze meant to inspire the respect afforded to the head of a family; the mother is more demurely turned to the side (a model of compliant femininity), while the child stares in fascination at the camera. (Author's collection)

and the results would not have been accurate. Some modern photographic restoration processes might show up unusual eye/skin combinations such as very white skin and dark eyes, or heterochromia (one blue and one brown eye), a condition that can be inherited and affects about one in 10,000 people. For the exact colour of your ancestor's eyes you will need to turn to written descriptions, such as those in prison records, transportation records, First World War service records and passports. There is more detail on all of these and how to access them in Chapter 5.

Our interest in our ancestors' eyes is pretty much guaranteed, but what, if anything, are we likely to find out?

PORTRAITS AND PHOTOGRAPHS

In the eighteenth century, portrait painters who could accurately represent the eyes of their subject were highly regarded. After all, portraits were painted in order to convey the personality, psychology and inward characteristics of the sitter as much as his or her external appearance, and this information was largely conveyed through the eyes. You should bear in mind, though, that portrait painters were tasked with the job of creating a positive picture of the sitter, so any less than attractive ocular characteristics, such as squints or heavy under-eye bags, would have been deliberately obscured or altered.

So highly prized were skilful painted representations of the eyes that a curious offshoot of the fashion for portrait painting developed. This was the so-called 'eye portrait' or 'lovers' eye' – a tiny painting of the eyes (or more often just one eye) of the subject, which could be concealed in a locket, brooch or ring. The fad for these peculiar little pictures was started in 1785 by George IV, who carried an eye portrait of his lover, Mrs Fitzherbert, apparently in order that her identity could be kept anonymous.

With the advent of popular photography in the mid-nineteenth century came a new challenge for those wishing to preserve images of the face. Photographic shutter times of many minutes required the subjects to keep their eyes open for extended periods – something that inevitably created an artificial stare in some early photographs, or alternatively a blur around the eye area when the subjects had blinked. Sometimes, in cases where a sitter had inadvertently closed his or her eyes, pupils would be painted on the photograph after the printing process was complete. With improvements in the collodion process, photographs became more accurate, more affordable and, portraits in particular, more popular. The first portrait photographer opened in London in 1841. By 1861 there were more than 200 such businesses in the capital.

Early photographic portraits (developed first in 1854 but popular in England from 1860) were made on *cartes de visite* or calling cards of 2¼in x 3½in mounted on a paper card of 2½in x 4in. Don't imagine that your ancestor entered the photographic studio and chose how to stand or which way to look. From mid century there were training manuals for photographers that advised them on how to deal with 'sitters', and it is highly likely that your ancestor was instructed by the photographer on all matters including the direction of his or her gaze. In many early photographs the direction of the gaze simply followed the direction of the head, but subtleties soon developed, and the direction of the gaze became, in many instances, part of an elaborate code, which often conveyed something about the status of the sitters and the event that was being commemorated.

Adult men, for example, were usually portrayed with a look that suggested strength, dignity or even nobility. Young women were instructed not to look straight at the camera to avoid appearing loose or brazen. There were exceptions; in some early documentary-style photographs Lancashire pit girls in their work clothes glare at the camera. In their case the straight stare remained uncorrected by the photographer, who perhaps wished to portray them as provocative, masculine and, perhaps most of all, lower class. But most other women looked aside in photographs – a pose that suggested demureness, modesty and even chastity. In keeping with Victorian ideas about women's supportive domestic role within a marriage, wives gazed adoringly (though never amorously) at their spouses. Widows and the bereaved looked down in exaggerated grief at bunches of flowers or photographs of the deceased to indicate their loss. Sometimes, of course, the photographer's careful instructions just didn't work: many sitters were baffled by the whole photographic process, and faced the camera with eyes that expressed a great deal of bashfulness and uncertainty.

The *cartes de visite* photographs of the mid-Victorian period gave way in the mid-1860s to the larger 'cabinet photographs' (the first, introduced by Marion and Co. in 1862, were 6¾in by 4½in). By the 1880s and 1890s head and shoulders vignette photographs – which eliminated the distraction of the hands or other parts of the body – were very popular. The essential character of the sitter was now suggested almost entirely by the facial characteristics, and particularly the eyes. Portrait photographs in the form of postcards appeared in about 1902. One of several popular photographic techniques was 'Rembrandt Lighting', which threw light on one side of the face while the other side was in shadow, in the manner of a Rembrandt painting. The shadowed side of the face characteristically included a triangle of light below the eye, no wider than the eye and no longer than the nose. The results were realistic but slightly dramatic portraits, in which emphasis was placed on the eyes. As society loosened up and technology improved from the Edwardian period onwards, the range of allowable emotions expressed by the eyes increased.

DATING A PORTRAIT OR PHOTOGRAPH FROM THE EYES

Surprisingly enough, the eyes might give us pointers to the date at which a painting was painted or a photograph taken.

SPECTACLES

Glasses for the eyes have a long history and have been worn by people of all classes since the thirteenth century. If your ancestor in a portrait or photograph is wearing spectacles, look carefully at the design. Bifocals, two lenses of different strengths joined across the middle, were in use from as early as the 1760s. Many early spectacles were handheld, and none had rigid sides or 'temples' until the late eighteenth century. And, even though they might have been deemed old-fashioned, spectacles that simply rested on the nose (so-called 'pince-nez') were commonly worn from the 1840s right through to the 1930s. Most spectacles of the nineteenth century had oval lenses. The terminals (ends of the sides) of spectacles moved through numerous designs during the eighteenth and nineteenth centuries; from spirals to rings (perhaps for use with a ribbon) and then ovals. Double-jointed sides arrived in the mid-eighteenth century.

From the early nineteenth century a whole range of eyewear became popularly available, including lorgnettes, eyeglasses and quizzing glasses, as well as the more familiar 'nose spectacles' and spectacles with sides of different kinds. After the development of wire-drawing in 1837, many spectacles were made from 'blued' steel. These were particularly popular in the 1850s and 1860s. Flexible curl sides (with attractive descriptions such as 'cable curl', 'comfort curl' and 'supercomfort cable curl') were popular in spectacles (especially those worn by children) from the 1850s onwards. Look carefully at the shape of the bridge of the spectacles: C shapes were joined by X, K, 'scroll' and 'crank' shapes as the nineteenth century progressed. Bridges shaped like a W (sometimes known as a 'saddlebridge') did not appear until the 1880s and were very fashionable in the early 1900s, partly because they contributed to a better cosmetic appearance by making the nose look shorter!

There were a number of noteworthy milestones in design. In 1797, so-called 'D-type' spectacles appeared. These had supplementary lenses that could be folded over the main lenses to give a choice of optical experiences. With the arrival of open-air railway travel in the 1840s a particular model of these, known as 'railway spectacles', was developed, which aimed to protect the eyes from sparks, steam and dust.

Rimless spectacles of different designs were available throughout the nineteenth century, but the so-called 'invisibles', with thin wire frames set into grooves in the lenses, did not appear until the end of the century. Although tinted lenses had long been worn as an eye-correcting device,

The Rev. A.J. Glendinning Nash, Vicar of St John the Evangelist, Bradford, 1897. Pince-nez spectacles like these, with their oval lenses, hard bridge, nose pads and chain, were very popular with middle-aged men between 1890 and 1900. By 1920 they were seen as befitting only the elderly. (Rev. A.J. Glendinning Nash, *Home Words For Heart and Hearth*, ed. Rev. Charles Bullock, 1897)

sunglasses as we know them today were first popular in the 1930s. For a much fuller description of the different kinds of spectacles worn in different historical periods, together with helpful images, see www.antiquespectacles. com/guide/guide_to_assist.htm.

EYE MAKE-UP

The presence of make-up around the eyes of your female ancestors may be another guide to dating portraits and photographs. In the late eighteenth century the 'made-up' look was highly artificial, with aristocratic ladies wearing white powder (often containing lead) on their faces, and sporting cheeks and lips coloured red with vegetable dyes and vinegar. The eyes were generally left undecorated, although eyebrows could be darkened and shaped, with the preferred style being full and semicircular. By the Victorian period, however, cosmetics of any kind were frowned upon for ladies and the middle classes. Heavy eye make-up in particular was seen as the provenance only of prostitutes or ladies of dubious morals. Many women, however, lined their eyes surreptitiously with candle soot or burnt matchsticks, and darkened their eyelashes with the melted wax of candles, applied with a needle or with beeswax. Pupils could always be artificially dilated and made to sparkle with a sprinkling of the juice of the deadly nightshade plant – hence its colloquial name 'bella donna' (the Italian for 'beautiful woman').

At the turn of the twentieth century commercial make-up was ready to make an assault on the senses of the female population. Mass publishing, made possible by advances in printing, led to a new emphasis on cosmetics in Edwardian magazines. The natural look was still favoured, but powder, rouge and eye make-up were once again as acceptable as they had first been over a hundred years earlier. The First World War (1914–18) brought increased financial independence for working-class women, and this in turn led to more cosmetics being bought and worn. In 1917 the London-based company Rimmel marketed the first packaged cosmetic mascara made from petroleum jelly and black coal dust. By the 1920s some prominent women were wearing distinctive heavy make-up. Queen Alexandra, wife of George V, for example, met with some public disapprobation because of her penchant for dark eye make-up. But it was probably not until the 1930s that the average woman started to use mascara, and not until the 1950s that she added eyeliner and eyeshadow.

The shape of women's eyebrows (arched, angled, curved or flat) may be another clue to the date of twentieth-century photographs. Eyebrows could change (just as fashions in make-up and dress changed) with the current trends. The straight, thin eyebrows of the 1920s gave way in the 1930s to eyebrows that were even thinner, with accentuated height and length creating a look of permanent surprise. Some women even shaved off their eyebrows during this decade and there was also a fashion for false eyelashes. In the 1940s it was back to a natural appearance for eyebrows, with a medium thickness, while the chic women of the 1950s created a look around thick, dark, angled brows.

EMOTIONAL STATE

A less scientific way of dating photographs, but one which all family historians are guilty of, is to look for evidence of an ancestor's well-being or emotional state in his or her eyes. It is tempting to interpret the look in the eyes in a particular photograph as evidence of our ancestor's reaction to a recent family event: downcast eyes being a possible testimony to the raw grief of widowhood or the loss of a child; wide-open eyes and expectant eyebrows signalling happier events such as a betrothal or anniversary. It has often been commented, for instance, that after Prince Albert's death in 1861, Queen Victoria's luminous blue eyes became sorrowful and always looked as if they were brimming with tears. These matters, of course, are pure speculation. Nevertheless, they can provide compelling corroboration of the date of an image.

EYES AND CHARACTER

As well as helping you to date a photograph, your ancestors' eyes may also signal deeper matters. There is still a commonly held belief that a person's character may be accessed through his or her eyes. In the Bible, Matthew (6: 22) comments that 'the light of the body is the eye'. And we are certainly wont to believe that our ancestors' eyes were indeed 'the windows to their souls', thus bright, open eyes seem to signal honesty and optimism, while close-set or squinting eyes somehow make us imagine ill temper and cruelty. More than any other facial feature, the eyes promise to tell us something of our ancestors' personalities and even their moral code.

These ideas are not merely the product of our wandering twenty-first-century imaginations. In the mid-nineteenth century there was a huge interest in the new pseudosciences of phrenology and physiognomy. Put simply, these fields of interest attributed mental characteristics to the shape of the skull and the characteristics of the face. The eyes were of supreme importance. If your ancestor had slightly protuberant ones, for example, his knowledgeable peers might have expected him to have 'a facility for language' and a very good memory. As an extension of this, ancestors with more distinctly bulging eyes with pouches and heavy eyelids might have been considered highly intelligent, if not geniuses. Phrenology and physiognomy had great credence in the first half of the nineteenth century, with people sometimes choosing their employees, spouses and friends on the basis of the shape of their skull and facial features!

By the end of the nineteenth century many of the phrenologists' and physiognomists' findings had been discredited, and their instruments and analysis were relegated to sideshows at the fairground or along the seaside promenade. Unhappily, however, some of the early ideas about connections between physical and moral characteristics were taken up by the budding proponents of criminal anthropology, and later eugenics. Towards the end of the Victorian era and well into the twentieth century 'experts' put forward the idea that those who had committed serious crimes were more likely to have certain physical characteristics – among which were bushy eyebrows that met across the nose and large eye sockets with deep-set eyes. The most dangerous of these theorists, of course, conflated racial or regional characteristics (particularly those of Jews and Irish immigrants) with negative moral characteristics.

EYE CONDITIONS AND BLINDNESS

With ophthalmology in its infancy in the nineteenth century, many eye conditions, including squints and glaucoma, remained untreated and may be apparent in your family portraits or photographs. If your ancestor was blind this may be indicated in a number of different ways, including closed eyes, whitened eyes, vacant stares, the use of dark glasses, thickened lenses, optical devices or blindfolds. For a fascinating gallery of portraits of people in the past suffering from eye conditions see www.commons.wikimedia. org/wiki/Category:Eye_problems_in_portrait_paintings. Blindness was

Pupils on the 1911 census at the Yorkshire School for the Blind, King's Manor, York. In the 'Infirmity' column they are described either as 'Totally blind' or 'Partially blind'. (www. findmypast.co.uk)

also sometimes indicated by pose. The sitter might point at or touch his own eyes, he might hold his hands outwards, or display open hands that scan and feel the air. Props such as a cane or a musical instrument might also indicate blindness, as might the presence of a helper, such as a child or a dog. A blind ancestor will not have acquired a white cane until after 1921 or a trained guide dog until after 1931.

If you suspect an ancestor was blind from a photograph, take a look at the record of your ancestor in one of the decennial censuses. Blindness was recorded in the last column of the 'Householders' Schedule' from 1851 onwards. By 1861 householders were required to enter either the term 'Blind' or 'Born Blind' – although people did not always adhere to this rule. A government report on this census enumerated the number of blind persons in the UK as 29,248, with the vast majority having become blind after birth. The report put the causes of blindness down to a combination of smallpox (the most significant factor), accidents, purulent ophthalmia (a disease affecting newborn babies) and, more sinisterly, 'the unhealthiness of dwellings, the want of cleanliness, bad or insufficient food, and other well-known causes of physical deterioration, as well as by every description of overwork involving a considerable strain on these organs of vision, whether that of the student, the needlewoman, or the mechanic'. The report also noted that blindness was much more common in Ireland than in other parts of the UK, and put this down to 'epidemic ophthalmia' – prevalent in the country for 160 years, and accentuated by the potato famine of 1845–52. Thousands of Irish peasants, pauper children and even soldiers were declared blind.

There was a common feeling in the nineteenth century that being blind was less of an affliction than being deaf (since blindness often led to an acuity of the other senses, whereas deafness was frequently accompanied by dumbness and consequent apparent idiocy). Nevertheless, the blind really struggled in Victorian Britain. Most of the help afforded them was from private charity in the form of schools, manufacturing establishments, societies and relief funds. But unfortunately many blind people languished in workhouses without the benefit of education or employment. The advantage of all this for the family historian is that you might find substantial details of the experiences of your blind ancestors in the records of any of these institutions. Check out their location at www.nationalarchives.gov.uk

THE DEAD

Finally, if you notice something particularly odd about the eyes of an ancestor in a photograph – either closed or with a vacant expression – consider that this might be because it was taken after he or she had died. The Victorians were fond of post-mortem photographs (an example of *memento mori*) as reminders or memories of the dead. In these pictures the recently deceased were often propped up and dressed as if alive. Their eyes might be artificially held open or, even more bizarrely, painted in (on the eyelid) after the photograph was printed. Long exposure times meant that images of the living (and moving) were often blurred. So if the image of one person in a photograph is unusually clear while those around him are blurred, it is a possibility that this is, in fact, a corpse!

FIND OUT MORE

Lorenzo Nile Fowler, *Handbook of Physiology, Phrenology and Physiognomy, Illustrated with a Descriptive Chart*, Forgotten Books, 2010.

Sharrona Pearl, *About Faces: Physiognomy in Nineteenth-Century Britain*, Harvard University Press, 2010.

Leslie A. Zebrowitz, *Reading Faces: Window to the Soul?* Perseus, 1997.

The MusEYEum: British Optical Association Museum, The College of Optometrists, 42 Craven Street, London, WC2N 5NG.

www.athro.com/evo/gen/inherit1.html – an explanation of how eye colours are inherited.

www.cogitz.com/2009/08/28/memento-mori-victorian-death-photos – Victorian post-mortem photographs.

www.college-optometrists.org – history of spectacles.

www.paranormal-encyclopedia.com/p/phrenology – the pseudoscience of phrenology.

www.visionofbritain.org.uk/text/chap_page.jsp?t_id=SRC_P&c_id=11&cpub_id=EW1861GEN&show=DB – report on the 1861 census of England and Wales relating to the blind and the deaf and dumb.

2

Down in the Mouth

TEETH

ave you ever wondered why your ancestors often look so downcast on photographs? One reason is perhaps because their teeth were in such a poor state. Rumour has it that while twentieth-century photographers asked their sitters to say 'cheese' and grin, their nineteenth-century counterparts preferred the word 'prunes', with very glum results.

TEETH IN PHOTOGRAPHS

There may be a number of explanations for the almost uniformly morose expressions in Victorian and Edwardian photographs. Showing the teeth was certainly considered to be a sign of low breeding and even obscenity a century and more ago. Women with open mouths or teeth showing were at risk of appearing sexually predatory. For men, revealing the teeth might detract from the dignity and manliness that most photographers wished to convey.

In keeping with these popular prejudices, commercial photographers across the country adopted a convention of portraying people with formal, unsmiling expressions. Long photographic exposure times (often while the head was held in a head clamp or brace) also meant that sitters were asked to keep their mouths shut to minimise movement. It has even been suggested that sitters were given the opium-based drug laudanum to keep them docile while photographs were taken.

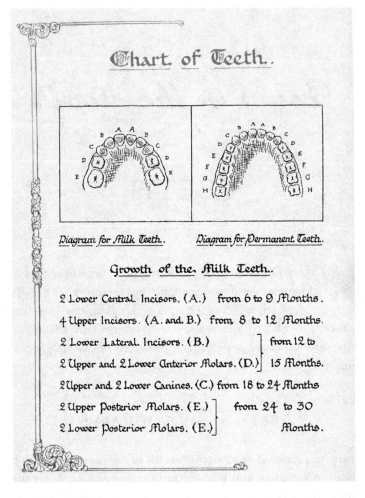

Chart of Teeth.

Diagram for Milk Teeth.   *Diagram for Permanent Teeth.*

Growth of the Milk Teeth.

2 Lower Central Incisors. (A.) from 6 to 9 Months.

4 Upper Incisors. (A. and. B.) from 8 to 12 Months.

2 Lower Lateral Incisors. (B.) ⎤ from 12 to

2 Upper and 2 Lower Anterior Molars. (D.) ⎦ 15 Months.

2 Upper and 2 Lower Canines. (C.) from 18 to 24 Months

2 Upper Posterior Molars. (E.) ⎤ from 24 to 30

2 Lower Posterior Molars. (E.) ⎦ Months.

By the 1920s mothers were expected to understand and take responsibility for the proper growth and care of their children's teeth, as this chart from a baby record book shows. (Lady Beecham, *Our Baby: A Mother's Companion and Record*, 1920)

But another, and probably equally important, reason for the morose looks was undoubtedly the generally poor condition of our ancestors' teeth. Without the benefit of braces, crowns, whiteners, veneers or dentures that fitted properly, keeping the mouth shut was probably a wise option for most. Even when photographic exposure times became considerably shorter, those who posed for photographs continued to keep their lips together.

THE STATE OF THE NATION'S TEETH

Those with strong, white teeth were in a fortunate minority in the nineteenth century, and this fact did not escape the attention of astute social commentators. Novelists such as Jane Austen (1775–1817) commented on the 'good' or at least 'tolerable' teeth of those who were to be her heroes and heroines, and the poor teeth of other – less worthy – characters. In printed media the state of a person's teeth could increasingly be viewed as a kind of barometer of their moral life – good teeth suggesting moral integrity and clean-living, and poor teeth intimating loose morals and even criminality.

Missing teeth, toothaches and cavities must have been a frequent aggravation and embarrassment for most of our ancestors. Queen Victoria herself suffered a great deal with her teeth, and was constantly calling upon her doctors to replace lost fillings and to create better dentures. Mrs Gaskell recorded in her biography that, as with many other young women of the times, novelist Charlotte Brontë's (1816–55) plain features were not helped by the fact that she had several missing teeth. Charlotte's sister Emily (1818–48) had protruding front teeth, which had been reduced to just one tooth by the end of her short life (she was only thirty when she died). Speculation that a recently discovered photograph may be of Charlotte, Emily and their third sister Anne is partly based upon the fact that the sitter believed to be Emily has a protruding front tooth, just visible when the photograph is enlarged.

Archaeological evidence points to the fact that Britain's teeth actually got worse during the nineteenth century. After a study of the skeletal remains in two graveyards in Ashton-under-Lyne, Lancashire, scientists have recently concluded that there were more caries (and more examples of other dental diseases such as calculus, periodontis and abscesses) in the teeth of those buried in the second half of the nineteenth century than the first. This indicates that our ancestors from the 1850s onwards were eating a softer, more carbohydrate-rich diet based on finely milled flour. More sugar was also eaten after the repeal of the import duty on sugar in 1846.

As well as being affected by diet, our male ancestors' teeth may have been heavily discoloured by pipe, cigar and (after the 1880s) cigarette smoking. A study by the Museum of London in 2011 of the skeleton remains of mid-century Victorians from a cemetery in Whitechapel revealed that many had teeth deformed by notches created by smoking a clay pipe. In some cases a complete circular hole was apparent when the upper and lower jaws were closed.

Before the Edwardian period few 'respectable' women smoked, but in the early twentieth century holding a cigarette became one of the many new expressions of a growing female emancipation, and nicotine-yellow teeth may well have bothered our female ancestors too.

TEETH AND HEALTH

If only we had access to our ancestors' teeth they could tell quite a story. Modern archaeological (or more precisely palaeopathological) research methods allow analysis of the chemical make-up or 'isotopic constituents' of teeth. Since these are laid down in childhood, it would be possible to tell where our ancestors grew up geographically and even how long they spent in a particular area. In addition, the enamel on teeth reflects periods of poor nutrition – indicative perhaps of class status – and also periods of ill health. It is possible to tell from a tooth, for example, that a child had several periods of ill health between say the ages of 7 and 11.

Of course, fascinating though this is, none of this information is going to be accessible to the ordinary family historian, but matters to do with teeth do sometimes turn up in written records. Tooth decay was not just a cosmetic matter in the past: it could cause illness and even death. 'Teething' was frequently given as a cause of death on infant death certificates. In fact it was not teething itself that caused death, rather the cutting of teeth; this could lead to infection of the gums, which could in turn lead to convulsions, diarrhoea and even death. It is also possible that teething infants who were being weaned might have ingested contaminated food or milk weakened with infected water, which might have led to fatal illness.

The death certificates of older people are less likely to give 'teeth' as a cause of death, but plenty of people died from septicaemia caused by gum disease and abscesses. One of the most famous of these was Josiah Wedgwood, the pottery manufacturer, who died in January 1795. A friend wrote that he was 'seized with a dreadful pain in his face and teeth', and a local doctor perceived that 'a slough or mortification' had begun in the mouth. Despite the attentions of the best medical practitioners of the day, Josiah died three weeks later. The friend reported that had he been a poor man he would not have lived more than three days.

The state of people's teeth could also betray worse health problems. Those suffering from congenital syphilis, for example, often had 'Hutchinson's

CERTIFIED COPY OF AN ENTRY OF DEATH

GIVEN AT THE **GENERAL REGISTER OFFICE**

Application Number ...COL312188...

REGISTRATION DISTRICT					Wigan			
...1866...DEATH in the Sub-district of ...Aspull...					...in the ...County of Lancaster...			

Columns:-	1	2	3	4	5	6	7	8	9
No.	When and where died	Name and surname	Sex	Age	Occupation	Cause of death	Signature, description and residence of informant	When registered	Signature of registrar
452	Twenty sixth February 1866 Dray Lane Aspull	Alice Fletcher	Female	1 year	Daughter of Lydia Fletcher weaver in a cotton factory	Teething 4 months Pneumonia 12 days Certified	X The mark of Lydia Fletcher Present at the death Dray Lane Aspull	No 1 Twenty eighth February 1866	William Clark Registrar	Superintendent W. L.

CERTIFIED to be a true copy of an entry in the certified copy of a Register of Deaths in the District above mentioned.

Given at the GENERAL REGISTER OFFICE, under the Seal of the said Office, the ...26th... day of ...July... 2007

DYB 608192

See note overleaf

CAUTION: THERE ARE OFFENCES RELATING TO FALSIFYING OR ALTERING A CERTIFICATE AND USING OR POSSESSING A FALSE CERTIFICATE ©CROWN COPYRIGHT
WARNING: A CERTIFICATE IS NOT EVIDENCE OF IDENTITY.

VHT

The cause of death given for 1-year-old Alice Fletcher in 1866 was 'teething' (four months) and 'pneumonia' (twelve days). (Author's collection)

teeth', distinctive screwdriver-shaped incisors that immediately gave away their life-threatening condition.

Despite the appalling lack of dental hygiene in Victorian Britain, teeth occupied something of a special place in the imagination of the nation, with a number of superstitious beliefs being popularly held. Babies born with teeth were thought, for example, to be heading for greatness, while women with wide-spaced teeth were assumed to be 'loose'. The milk teeth of children were often kept for sentimental reasons and incorporated into household artefacts. Some people had jewellery made out of them – so look out for rings and bracelets with unusual white stones! When Queen Victoria's eldest daughter, Princess Victoria, the Princess Royal, lost her first tooth while visiting Ardverikie by Loch Laggan in 1847, her father Prince Albert, who had pulled the tooth out, had it incorporated into a brooch for her mother. This item of jewellery was designed in gold and enamel, shaped like a thistle, with the little white tooth, set in gold, as its blossom. Later, Queen Victoria had a bracelet made out of the teeth of all nine of her children.

A BRIEF HISTORY OF DENTAL CARE

The first comprehensive guide to dentistry, *Le Chirurgien Dentiste*, was written by a Frenchman, Pierre Fauchard, in 1728. This included everything that was known at the time on dental disease and how to deal with it. However, it was a long time before these ideas filtered down to most of our ancestors in the ordinary population.

Early dentistry concentrated on the alleviation of pain rather than on preventative work. The only quick and sure solution for toothache was to extract the tooth. Up until the 1850s problems with teeth were dealt with by extraction or through the use of herbal remedies. Many people just learnt to live with the pain and infections that resulted from poor teeth. There were also a number of well-tried home remedies for toothache, such as these suggested in *The Sunlight Year Book* as late as 1898:

> When arising solely from a hollow tooth, toothache may be cured by a few drops of chloroform on a piece of cotton wool pressed into the cavity, or a paste may be made of cayenne pepper and brandy or whiskey and pressed into the hollow. Quinine may be taken as an internal remedy, and the tooth should be stopped by a competent dentist.

Early findings by the British scientist Humphrey Davy in 1800 suggested that 'laughing gas', or nitrous oxide, might be effective in curing dental pain. Further studies by the American Horace Wells in the 1840s, in which he used nitrous oxide as an anaesthetic during a tooth extraction, proved inconclusive, and our ordinary ancestors had to wait until much later before they were commonly able to enjoy general anaesthetic for tooth extractions. Local anaesthetics were possible from 1884, but unavailable to most patients.

Gruesome extraction instruments (known as 'pelicans' or 'keys') were replaced by the kinder forceps in the 1860s; nevertheless, a trip to the dentist continued to be an unpleasant experience. Patients frequently had to be held down in the dental chair, with an employee being paid specifically for this purpose. After an extraction the resulting gaps in the teeth were

Nineteenth-century dentistry was not quite as rudimentary as this cartoon from 1830 would have us believe. But without proper methods of pain relief, the horrors of having a tooth pulled were very real. (Illustration from William Rodgers Richardson (writing as Graham Everitt), *English Caricaturists and Graphic Humourists of the Nineteenth Century*; engraving by George Cruikshank, captioned 'The Dentist', 1830)

most often simply left to heal over, but sometimes substitute teeth (from living donors) were available. From the early 1800s fillings were made from a variety of materials from tin to gold; many included mercury, which at the time was not considered to be harmful. In time, a foot-operated drill speeded up the process of filling.

If your ancestors appear to have had a good set of teeth, beware: they may have been false. Dentures were big business in the Victorian period. Generally poorly fitting and uncomfortable to wear, they had traditionally been made from an odd miscellany of materials such as whalebone and wood. From 1774 porcelain dentures were made. These tended to look unnaturally white, and often chipped and broke. In the 1820s Claudius Ash, a goldsmith practising in Westminster, London, began mounting porcelain dentures on gold plates. Romantic poet William Wordsworth (1770–1850) had been proud of his own teeth, but finally succumbed to a false set. These he took out in the evening, much to the annoyance of visitors, such as the writer Harriet Martineau. She complained that she could not understand much of what he said when he was not wearing his teeth, and she consequently took to calling on him earlier in the day. Interestingly, when Wordsworth had his portrait painted he was asked to take out his false teeth, as the photographer thought that they distorted the shape of his face.

There was an active trade in teeth from humans and other animals, which could be fitted into dentures of one sort or another. Dentists might acquire teeth from a number of sources, including the mouths of the poor, who were sometimes paid for giving up their molars. Judges sometimes allowed the teeth of executed criminals to be pulled from their mouths, and the teeth of dead and unidentified paupers could also legally be used. Other surprising sources of teeth were the corpses of young men who had fallen in various battlefields during the Napoleonic period. These were popularly known as 'Waterloo Teeth', and were often worn with pride, by those who could afford them, right through the nineteenth century.

From the 1840s onwards artificial teeth started to replace real ones in dentures. In the 1850s vulcanite dentures (made from a kind of rubber that could be moulded to suit the exact shape of the wearer's mouth) with porcelain dentures inserted were introduced. These tended to be better fitting but were difficult to clean, slightly porous and could irritate the gums – all of which made them less than ideal. Our ancestors who had false teeth in the Victorian period would have worn them only for cosmetic reasons. They were not suitable for dining.

When it came to caring for their own teeth, our ancestors had a bewildering choice of powders and potions to choose from, if they had the money to do so. Tooth powders or 'dentifrice' became available in the eighteenth century. These had a base of bicarbonate of soda, but they could also include abrasives such as brick dust, cuttlefish, crushed china or earthenware and even sugar. Borax was added at the end of the eighteenth century to produce a foaming effect.

Powders became pastes in the early nineteenth century, when glycerine was added. Soap was introduced into toothpaste in 1824 and chalk in the 1850s. In 1873 toothpaste was mass-produced, sweet smelling and sold in a jar for the first time. An American manufacturer put toothpaste in a collapsible tub in 1892. As for toothbrushes, they had been around (replacing toothpicks) since about 1780. The first mass-produced ones were made by British manufacturer William Addis, with handles carved from cattle bones and bristles made from wild boar or horse hair. These were beyond the means of most of the population, who probably used frayed sticks or their fingers.

Teeth were whitened with burnt bread or charcoal and flossed, after 1815, with a piece of silk thread (advocated by American Dr Levi Spear Parmly). The importance of teeth cleaning was understood by military nurse Florence Nightingale (1820–1910), who always took a stack of toothbrushes with her on military duties. In 1898 *The Sunlight Year Book*, published by Lever Brothers, had some rather archaic advice for cleaning the teeth, which understandably mentioned its own product, Sunlight Soap, more than once:

> The proper care of the teeth is most important. Children should early be taught the effective use of the tooth-brush, and nothing is better for cleaning the teeth than soap. Rub a soft tooth-brush over a piece of Sunlight Soap and then thoroughly brush the teeth on both sides, night and morning, both on retiring to rest and on rising. Tartar should never form on them with this treatment; but if it should have formed before the continued use of soap, a little powdered cuttle-fish bone may be permitted.

After 1850 the rising middle classes in the industrial cities began to demand better dental care, and the emphasis shifted from surgical cures to preventative action. The Dental Act of 1878 required dentists to take a qualification – the Licence in Dental Surgery (LDS) – and to register. In practice, however, even though there were more qualified dentists around at the end of the nineteenth century, few people could afford to use them.

By the Edwardian period it was generally understood that teeth cleaning was essential for good health. Brushes made from horsehair were used, as well as a vast array of toothpastes and powders. Many mouthwashes were available. These, including Listerine (developed in the 1890s), sometimes doubled up as an aftershave and as a gargle to combat germs. In the twentieth century, false teeth came to be made from synthetic resins and were much better fitted to the shape of the mouth as well as more resilient. Fluoride was added to toothpaste as a deterrent to tooth decay in 1914, and after the Second World War synthetic detergents were added. Toothbrushes were made from nylon from the late 1930s, with electric toothbrushes not being easily available until the 1960s.

RESEARCHING ANCESTORS WHO
WERE DENTISTS

If your ancestor ran a dental practice you may find a reference or advertisement in a trade directory. Many of these are freely searchable by keyword at www.historicaldirectories.org. Hard copies can usually be found in local libraries.

You can find out more about a dentist ancestor from the annual Dentists' Registers, started in 1879 and held by the British Dental Association. The registers record those dentists who received the Licence in Dental Surgery (LDS) qualification from the Royal College of Surgeons (available from 1860), and those others who could prove that they had been involved in the bona fide practice of dentistry before 1878. The registers record the first and last date of registration as a dentist, the dentist's qualification and the institution from which it was obtained, the address of the dental practice and the dates at which the practitioner changed address. But be careful: between 1878 and 1921 there were a large number of unregistered dental practitioners whose names will not appear in the registers. It was only after the Dentists' Act of 1921 that the practice of dentistry was firmly limited to qualified dentists.

You won't find any women dentists in the early registers. Although many women have practised as dentists throughout history, the first British woman to formally qualify was Lilian Murray, in Edinburgh in 1895. It was actually another twenty years before women in England were admitted to an LDS course.

Ancestors who were working as dentists before 1879 may be more difficult to trace. These practitioners may have trained through informal apprenticeship arrangements, and it is possible that records may be held in local record offices. You can search the contents of all local archives through the website of the National Archives, www.nationalarchives.gov.uk.

The British Dental Museum will search (for a small donation) for obituaries or other possible articles about your dentist ancestors in the dental press. Email the museum at museum@bda.org, stating the full name of your ancestor, their birth and death dates if known (or rough dates) and the area of the country in which you think they lived and worked.

As a result of all these improvements in dental practice together, of course, with a speeding up of photographic exposure times and a generally more relaxed manner of living, your ancestors are far more likely to be smiling and showing their teeth in photographs from the Edwardian period onwards!

FIND OUT MORE

Gill Munton, *The Victorian Dentist*, OUP, 2002.

Angus Trumble, *A Brief History of the Smile*, Basic Books, 2003.

John Woodforde, *The Strange Story of False Teeth*, Routledge and Kegan Paul, 1968.

www.bda.org/museum – Museum of the British Dental Association, London.

thequackdoctor.com/index.php/tag/tooth-decay – some quack cures for tooth decay in history.

www.dentalmuseum.org – American National Museum of Dentistry, which has text and images relating to British dental history.

www.mddus.com/mddus/resource-library/2012/soundbite-05/written-in-the-bones%E2%80%A6-and-teeth.aspx – on scientific research of ancestral teeth and bones.

3

Their Crowning Glory

HAIR

air – and even the lack of it – is one of the most obvious aspects of our visual appearance that can link us to previous generations. You may have been told that you have hair of exactly the same colour and texture as your grandmother, or that you wear your parting just as your great uncle always did. Widow's peaks, cowlicks and double crowns are all inherited aspects of our appearance. But your ancestors' hair may be of interest to you regardless of any genetic similarities that you share.

HAIR IN PHOTOGRAPHS

The way your ancestors wore their hair when they posed for the painter or the camera may give you clues to the date at which the photograph was taken.

After the loose, tousled, Grecian styles of the Regency period (usually loosely defined as 1795–1837), men's hair got shorter in the second half of the nineteenth century, with cuts finishing just over the ears in 1850 and hair being much more closely cropped to the head by 1900. In the 1870s a centre parting running all the way from the forehead to the nape of the neck was also fashionable. Baldness, a characteristic that runs in families, was not enthusiastically embraced. Theories about what caused it ranged from hats, which were presumed to be too tight, to 'microbes' (identified at a meeting of the Dermatological Society of Paris in 1897) spread by dirty combs and brushes. There were numerous restorative cures advertised on the market for baldness in the Victorian period. In addition, vigorous rubbing of the head, tinctures made from vinegar and later vacuum caps and electric shock therapy were recommended. The complicated issue of the history of men's facial hair will be dealt with in the next chapter.

In the Regency period women also wore their hair modelled on Greek and Roman styles. Usually, the hair was worn up and fastened in a bun (which was often braided), with the front curled into soft ringlets. Partings were in the shape of a T, V, Y or U. Hats, bonnets and turbans were commonly worn, as were ribbons and combs. The early Victorian period

For help with dating a photograph, look out for the presence of braids, plaits, snoods and coils in the hair of your ancestors, as well as any kind of hair ornamentation. (*The Girl's Own Paper*, 1888)

saw a fashion for simpler styles. When Queen Victoria arrived for her first visit to Aberdeen in 1848 the plainness of the way in which her hair was braided aroused comment, but was soon copied. In very early photographs taken between 1845 and 1860 you will find women wearing their hair in plain, 'French' styles, characteristically smoothed back into a bun from a central parting with their ears covered. An alternative early style had the hair dangling in side ringlets with a bun at the back. The emphasis was on health, hygiene and natural beauty.

In the mid-Victorian period there was a fashion for fringes of various kinds, including the very popular 'Princess Alexandra Fringe', and ears were sometimes exposed. This period also saw the arrival of more ornate hairstyles (including the occasional use of artificial hair), with the hair at the back of the head allowed to hang loose, sometimes in ringlets, sometimes in large loops, emulating the complex folds that characterised the backs of skirts in these decades. The year 1872 saw the invention of crimpers (or 'ondulation tongues'), by Frenchman Marcel Grateau, with which the hair could be waved. The 1880s saw higher hairstyles (commonly known as the 'Pompadour' style), in which the hair was swept up from the forehead. The last decade of the nineteenth century saw a return to the bun – sometimes known as a 'psyche knot' – and fringes became less usual. Hair might also be worn in a loop or coil at the back of the head.

In the early twentieth century the variety of possible styles increased. Hair pads (known as 'rats') and frames allowed the hair of wealthy women to be piled high on the head in the classic Empire style of the Edwardian era. Plumes and ornamentation gave the appearance of even greater height and volume when the wearers went out at night. The permanent wave was invented byin 1905 German hairdresser Charles Nessler, using borax paste and electrically heated curlers, but this was far too expensive and laborious a process to really catch on at that time.

With the vote, and some degree of emancipation for women after the First World War, hairstyles for women became more daring. The bob – straight or waved – was fashionable in the 1920s. There was the invention of the 'cold wave' in 1938 by Arnold F. Willatt – an affordable and less time-consuming perming method that eventually became the favourite of the masses. Glamorous longer styles with curls, following the fashions of film stars, characterised the mid-1940s post-war period.

Hair in photographs can alert you to aspects of your family history other than just the date. The way your ancestor wore his or her hair at particular

Women's hairstyle choices have always been conditioned by money, sexual politics and contemporary fashion. Here are some fashionable styles of March 1888. (*The Girl's Own Paper*, 1888)

times during his or her life may also help you to work out how old he or she was when particular shots were taken. Some women in the 1920s cut their hair short when they started work, for example.

Hairstyles can even alert you to the class to which your ancestor belonged. Working-class women in the early twentieth century, for example, could not afford the pads or frames of false hair that created the volume and height of the styles worn by their middle- and upper-class sisters, nor could they afford to visit a hairdresser. Hair that has not been styled in any obvious way is a sure-fire clue to the poverty of your ancestors.

The styling of the hair often indicates age, with younger sisters wearing their locks down (loose or in ringlets known as 'barley' or 'sugar' curls), whilst their elder sisters wore it up. (*The Girl's Own Paper*, Vol. VIII, No. 359, 13 November 1886, *The Leisure Hour Office*, 1886)

REAL HAIR

Hairstyles in photographs may speak volumes, but it is much more exciting to discover actual locks of hair from the heads of your ancestors. You may be surprised at the number of different places that preserved hair has turned up among family belongings. Lockets worn around the neck in the nineteenth century sometimes conceal a swatch of hair, or the entwined hair of lovers. Mourning rings may include compartments containing a lock of the deceased's hair. Be careful when opening such items of jewellery: the hair may not be immediately obvious, as it may, for example, be pasted to the back of a photograph or portrait. Family history researchers have also found hair in silver snuff boxes and the backs of picture frames. Be careful not to jump to conclusions about your findings, however: the strands may not be hair at all, but rather some sort of cotton or rayon thread. To find out, take a small amount and burn it with a lit match. Wool and hair will burn with a splutter and the strands will fuse black. There will also be the unmistakable smell of burning hair.

In the nineteenth century some jewellery – bracelets, necklaces and brooches – was actually made entirely out of hair. This jewellery – known as hairwork – was particularly popular in America (see the website of the American Hairwork Society: www.hairworksociety.org). The hair of family members was sometimes woven into pictures and kept in display or picture frames. One contributor to the Hairwork Society website describes a 'hair album' of 1865, which was passed down through her family. In this, hair was braided, woven, stitched or embroidered into the page. Each sample was accompanied by a poem and the name of the family member contributing the hair. The album contained hair samples from over eighty different family members.

HAIR TO MARK BIRTHS, LOVE AFFAIRS AND DEATHS

Many locks of hair from previous centuries lie among collections of personal papers in archives up and down the country. They are contained in envelopes and wallets and lie tucked between the pages of diaries and letters. They range in date from a lock belonging to one John Freston who died in 1594, which is kept in the Normanton All Saints Parish Records at West Yorkshire Archive Service, Wakefield, to early twentieth-century examples; and in size from small snippings contained within ornamental pins to a long plait of hair believed to have belonged to Marianne Stafford Jerningham (*née* Smythe), who died in 1859, kept in the Staffordshire Record Office. These many preserved locks attest to the fact that the cutting and keeping of hair was an important ritual for our ancestors, marking those turning points in life so close to the heart of family history researchers – namely births, courtships and deaths.

Archival clippings would suggest that the locks from a baby's first haircut were often kept and sent to favourite relatives. Among the papers of the Middleton family (baronets of Belsay Castle) at the Northumberland Record Office, for example, is a lock of hair that is marked 'with Baby's love to Aunt Netty, 19th April, 1824'.

Sexual attraction was also marked by the preservation of hair. English literature has many examples of men taking women's hair as an expression of their love or as an act of betrothal; but in poetry and novels the act is rarely straightforward or pleasant. Alexander Pope's epic poem *The Rape of the Lock* (1712) is about just that – the cutting of a piece of hair from the head of a young lady without her permission. The poem is based on a real incident when Lord Petre (a friend of Pope's) cut off a piece of Lady Arabella Fermor's hair during a boat ride on the Thames near Hampton Court. The incident supposedly caused a rift between two of the wealthiest Catholic families in England at the time. And in Jane Austen's *Sense and Sensibility* (1811), when the rogue Willoughby obtains a lock of hair from the gentle Marianne, it would seem that their engagement is assured. In fact nothing could be further from the truth, and the taking of the hair becomes a symbol of Willoughby's dishonourable intentions.

Real life love affairs were also marked by gifts of hair. In King's College Archive Centre, Cambridge, among the papers of one George Humphrey Wolferstan Rylands, is a locket (from 1903) that contains a studio portrait of the head and shoulders of a young girl named Hester and (on the reverse) a lock of her hair. Hair was often exchanged between lovers as part of the courtship process. The Lincolnshire Archive includes the personal papers of a Lady Henrietta Scott, and among them a lock of hair wrapped in paper and inscribed 'my beloved Temple's hair 21st July, 1828'.

Hair was often sent between female friends and family members as a means of expressing affection, especially when one party had gone to live at a distance after marriage. In the eighteenth century Londoner Mary Bunnell sent her sister Sarah Kenrick (who was living in Cheshire) a lock of her hair. Sarah wrote back that she would 'wear it with pleasure', but that it would 'never appear so well as when on the head it came from'.

Locks of hair were also customarily taken from deceased relatives expressly for the purpose of providing comfort to those who survived them. This happened particularly in the case of the deaths of children. Among papers relating to the family of baby Anthony Hamond of Westacre, Norfolk (who died in 1783), for example, are a bodice and a lock of his hair (Norfolk Record Office). One of the largest archival collections of locks of hair is among the Harford family papers at the Bristol Record Office. Within this collection is a lock accompanied by a touching message: 'This paper contains some Hair of my beloved Husband – how valued by his widow Mary Harford.'

If a family member died abroad, it was usual for a clipping of hair to be taken and sent to the relatives back home. In the Hampshire Record Office the diaries of Emma Austen-Leigh include a lock of hair enclosed in paper with the words: 'My brother – dearest Drummond's hair cut off ... after his death at Palermo, 5th November 1832.' Likewise, among the papers of the Venables family of Oswestry, Shropshire, are a number of items relating to the death on 22 March 1887 of Olive Mary Venables in a railway accident in Burma. One of these is a lock of her hair.

HAIR AND HERO WORSHIP

Hair carried an enormous mystique in the nineteenth century – to the extent that ordinary people were prepared to pay good money for a snippet from the head of their favourite heroes. One example of this is the case of Grace Darling, the daughter of the keeper of the Longstone Lighthouse on the Farne Islands, who, on 7 September 1838, rescued five survivors of the wrecked ship, the *Forfarshire*, from a reef in the North Sea. News of Darling's bravery travelled fast and she soon became a national heroine. In the weeks and months following the event, pedlars in the north of England capitalised upon it by selling locks of what purported to be her hair.

The same desire to be connected with exceptional people prompted the 'fans' of Victorian novelists, poets, actors and singers to bombard them with requests for locks of their hair – all this in much the same way that celebrities nowadays are asked for their autograph. In hopeful mood, fans would send their idols locks of their own hair in exchange. The poet Lord Byron (1788–1824) received gifts of hair from over 100 lovers during his lifetime, and many of these have been kept in the archives of the publishing house John Murray (now in the National Library of Scotland). Locks from the head of Lady Caroline Lamb – one of Byron's better-known lovers – are stored here in an envelope labelled 'Caro Lamb hair'. Lamb is said to have cut off her tresses in order that she might better resemble the Cambridge choirboy whom Byron had seduced after forsaking her. In return for offerings of hair from would-be lovers, Byron sent back clippings of what he claimed to be his own hair. In fact, much of this came not from his own head but from the coat of his Newfoundland dog, Boatswain!

HAIR AND SCIENTIFIC TESTING

Today, hair is one of several bodily substances that potentially could be tested to prove or disprove a relationship between yourself and an ancestor, or even to find out more about an ancestor's general health.

There have been a few noteworthy scientific examinations of locks of hair in the recent past. A hank of Beethoven's crowning glory was taken from his head just after his death in March 1827 by a young music student named Ferdinand Hiller. In 1994 – after a number of peregrinations – this same lock of hair (encased in a glass frame) found its way to Sotheby's auction house, where it was purchased by two Americans. It had long been suggested that Beethoven's chronic ill health might have helped to stimulate his musical creativity; now, with a real piece of the great composer available for scientific analysis, a serious attempt was made to discover what diseases he might have suffered from. Forensic scientists discovered that the hair contained no traces of either mercury (commonly used to treat syphilis) or morphine (used as a general painkiller). More surprisingly, some of the tested strands of hair contained an unprecedentedly high amount of lead. This suggested that he might have suffered from a disease known as plumbism (caused by lead poisoning). Beethoven certainly suffered from gastrointestinal distress, gout, headaches and deafness – all of which are symptoms of plumbism. Here, for once, a lock of hair rather than a piece of written evidence may have shed light on one of the world's most intriguing historical puzzles.

However, the hair of your ancestor that you might come across in a Victorian locket or wallet is unlikely to yield much useful information. Unless a follicle is attached, hair does not contain the YDNA that comes from the male line of your family. Additionally, hair that has been preserved in jewellery will probably have been lovingly fondled over the years, and may thus be contaminated by the DNA of the person or people who have touched it. Contamination from soap residue is another problem.

On the positive side, hair does contain the mtDNA (mitochondrial DNA) that can tell you something about your maternal heritage. If you wanted to check that the hair in your mourning ring is actually that of your great-grandmother, you could have it examined and compared with that of a living female relative. By doing this, you could establish that the two donors were related, though not exactly what the relationship was.

At the moment, however, organisations that offer to test your DNA for genealogical reasons generally use swabs taken from the inside of the mouth, rather than hair samples. This is because the testing of hair samples is a very expensive process and one that is currently undertaken not by genealogists but by forensic scientists after a murder or other crime. Hold on to your hair samples, however. In the future, genealogical organisations might well commonly offer to test hair as well as saliva.

FIND OUT MORE

Georgine de Courtais, *Women's Hats, Headdresses and Hairstyles*, Dover Publications, 2006.

Russell Martin, *Beethoven's Hair: An Extraordinary Historical Odyssey and a Scientific Mystery Solved*, Broadway, 2001.

Victoria Sherrow, *Encyclopedia of Hair: A Cultural History*, Greenwood Press, 2006.

www.costumegallery.com/hairstyles.htm – hairstyle history from the Costume Library Research Gallery.

www.erasofelegance.com/fashion/hairstyles.html – hairstyles through the ages.

www.hairworksociety.org – website of the American Hairwork Society, which brings together people interested in the art of hairwork.

4

By the Hairs on his Chin

BEARDS

*M*en in nineteenth- and early twentieth-century family photographs often appear a little remote behind masses of facial hair. While your great-grandfather might have been bewhiskered, your grandfather might have sported sideburns and a handlebar moustache, and your father might, mysteriously, always have been clean-shaven. Strange as it may seem, these looks were not just individual fashion choices as they mostly are today, but matters that had much to do with the time and culture in which your male ancestors lived.

It is easy to unwittingly make all sorts of assumptions about an ancestor's life and character simply because he didn't use a razor. His glorious beard might suggest an outdoor life, rude health and virility, or sporting interests, for example. It might additionally indicate that he was wise, knowledgeable or of high social status. Less positively, that bushy growth might suggest that your ancestor was secretive, shy, devious, eccentric, villainous, or just plain unkempt.

The kind of beard sported by your ancestor might give away something about his personal qualities and his desire to keep up with the prevailing fashions of the day; but, more importantly, perhaps it may also tell you something more about the times in which he was living and his position within his community. At various points in their history beards have signified a variety of cultural characteristics including age, community tradition, military rank, religious affiliation and marital status.

Today there are a number of labels for describing beards that may prove useful to you as you investigate your ancestor or describe him to others.

The Rev. J. Arthur Robinson, 1897. Beards were traditionally worn by the clergy, sporting men, explorers, adventurers and all who embraced the outdoor life. (Rev. Charles Bullock, ed., *Home Words for Heart and Heart*, 1897)

A 'full' beard is downward flowing, usually with an integrated moustache. The 'chinstrap' is a beard with long sideburns that comes forward and ends under the chin, resembling a chinstrap. The 'goatee' is a tuft of hair grown on the chin; if accompanied by a moustache, this is known as a 'Van Dyck', after the painter Anthony Van Dyck (1599–1641). The 'Garibaldi' is a wide, full beard with rounded bottom and integrated moustache, named after the Italian general and politician Giuseppe Garibaldi (1807–82). A 'Verdi' is a short beard with a rounded bottom and a prominent moustache, named after the composer Giuseppe Verdi (1813–1901), while a 'neck beard' sees the chin and jawline shaven, leaving hair to grow only on the neck. There are many other kinds of beard.

A BRIEF HISTORY OF BEARDS

It might surprise you to know that many of the fashionable forebears who preceded your hairy Victorian ancestors will have been clean-shaven. Indeed, at times in the distant past beards have been negatively regarded as too aristocratic, too vulgar, too foreign, too 'philosophic' or too symptomatic of radicalism. From portraits we know that most European men of the upper classes were unbearded in the fifteenth century. In the sixteenth century clergymen were usually clean-shaven, but after the Protestant Reformation many grew their beards to indicate that they no longer held to the tenets of the Catholic Church. The longer the beard, the more revolutionary the wearer was considered to be.

In the late sixteenth and early seventeenth centuries beards enjoyed a spate of popularity. Henry VIII had established a tax on beards in 1535, and this was reintroduced by Queen Elizabeth I (r.1558–1603). Nevertheless, many popular shapes were worn during her reign including the 'Spanish spade beard', the 'English square-cut beard', 'the forked beard' and the 'stiletto beard'. In the seventeenth and eighteenth centuries beards fell out of fashion among the urban elite – although it is worth remembering that poor men will always have worn beards.

Beards started to become fashionable again for all classes of men during the Napoleonic Era (1799–1815). Indeed, in France, soldiers who had fought for Napoleon were patriotically referred to as 'Vieux Moustaches' (Old Moustaches), while younger men were forbidden to grow them. In the early years of the nineteenth century the fashion for wearing a beard spread across the Channel. Beards returned to Britain initially as a badge of honour for artists and political radicals, such as Chartists, but by the mid-nineteenth century they were moving back into the mainstream.

After 1850 massive beards, cantilevered moustaches and large, luxuriant sideburns (hair grown from the temples down the cheeks toward the jawline) became popular, particularly in London where fashions were set for much of the rest of the world. Sideburns were named after the American Colonel Burnside (a commander in the American Civil War, 1861–65), but in England they also had the nickname 'mutton chops' or 'Piccadilly weepers'. Your Victorian ancestor's beard may have come in one of a number of shapes and sizes and, even then, different models had different names. The most popular were the 'Franz Josef', long side-whiskers merging into a moustache, named after the Emperor of Austria (1830–1916), and the

'Imperial', a pointed tuft of whiskers on the chin named after Napoleon III (1808–73). Other beards aped the fashion set by other eminent statesmen, military men and cultural figures such as Charles Dickens (1812–70) and Benjamin Disraeli (1804–81). Many nineteenth-century European monarchs also had beards, including Alexander III of Russia (1845–94) and Frederick III of Germany (1831–88).

WHY YOUR ANCESTOR MIGHT HAVE WORN A BEARD

In the middle of the nineteenth century dramatic changes were afoot in men's appearance. Facial hair became more desirable and was a 'look' supported by new scientific knowledge. Frederick Knight Hunt wrote an article, 'Man Magnified', for the popular magazine *Household Words* (edited by Charles Dickens), in September 1851. He had studied the composition of human hair under a microscope, and had concluded that the shaving of a man's facial hair was plain unnatural:

> The razor, day by day, cuts [the beard] across; it cannot grow longer, so it grows thicker and stronger; and each slice taken away by the matutinal shave, looks, under the microscope, like a section of a bone; just as a bone is cut across when a ham is cut up into slices for broiling; whilst the *stump* remaining on the chin has just the same look as the bone on the section of grilled ham ready for the breakfast-table. The primly shaved mouth is thickly dotted round by myriads of hideous hair-stumps, with inner layer and marrow all exposed.

Surprisingly enough, a great number of newspaper articles and papers discussed the pros and cons of shaving around the years 1853 and 1854. In this debate the anti-shaving movement (sometimes referred to as the Beard Movement, although it was not an organised political campaign) had the upper hand.

The difference between being bearded and being clean-shaven became a matter of pride, patriotism, virility and class. Beards were an important part of the new and more masculine look of the Victorian male. For many men, being clean-shaven was starting to be seen as a sign of effeminacy. Industrialisation had brought many men from rural areas into the towns, exchanging agricultural jobs for office jobs. With this transition to non-physical indoor labour, they had shaved their chins. By growing back a beard, urban workers could symbolically claim back their lost masculinity. In May 1857 the writer Edmund Saul Dixon wrote, also in *Household Words*:

> Take a fine man of forty, with a handsome round Medicean beard … look at him well, so as to retain his portrait in your mind's eye; and then shave him close, leaving him, perhaps, out of charity, a couple of mutton-chop whiskers, one on each cheek, and you will see the humiliating difference. And if you select an old man of seventy for your experiment, and convert a snowy-bearded head that might sit for a portrait in a historical picture, into a close-scraped weazen-faced visage, like an avaricious French peasant on his way to haggle for swine at a monthly *franc-marché*, the descent from the sublime to the ridiculous is still more painfully apparent.

Masculinity apart, there were a number of cultural reasons why more men wore beards from the 1850s onwards. From other clues you might have about your ancestor's life, you might be able to work out which of the considerations below is likely to have caused him to wear a beard.

Many arguments were put forward to suggest that shaving was actually dangerous to health. It was thought that by accidentally cutting his face with a razor, a man could introduce potentially fatal infections. Beards and moustaches were thought to protect the lungs from the respiratory diseases (including tuberculosis) that plagued industrial cities. They also kept the neck and face warm, thus fending off sore throats and colds. Some nineteenth-century journalists even occasionally suggested that wearing a beard could help prevent facial cancers and blindness!

Ancestors who were in the British military from the Crimean War (1854) onwards tended to be hirsute, and their heroic image was something that the ordinary man on the street wanted to copy. If the ancestor in your photograph really was a military man, take particular note of the shape of his beard or moustache, as the style of these may help you work out his rank. In general, the bushier the beard and the larger the moustache, the more senior your ancestor will probably have been. From the 1860s until the middle of the First World War a moustached ancestor might well have been in the army: military men were actually forbidden to shave their upper lips during this period. The regulation was finally abolished on 6 October 1916 by an Army Order issued by Lieutenant-General Sir Nevil Macready, Adjutant-General to the Forces, who readily shaved off his own moustache

– which he apparently hated. Since then, men in the Royal Navy have been allowed to wear 'full sets', that is beards and moustaches joined, but not beards or moustaches alone. The other forces (Army, Royal Air Force and Royal Marines) allow moustaches only (except where beards are being worn for religious reasons).

Ancestors who were colonial administrators wore beards as part of an unofficial but widely recognised Imperial uniform. The mid-nineteenth century was a period during which Britain's imperial power was at its height. Administrators in outposts across the world had a sort of uniformity of dress and demeanour. For inspiration in their government of foreign peoples, they looked back to their bearded Anglo-Saxon and Viking ancestry (a genealogy that clearly separated them from the rest of the world). British soldiers in India had an added imperative for growing facial hair; their Indian subjects, who wore moustaches as a sign of virility, might have mocked their Imperial overlords had they not followed suit.

If your male ancestors were especially religious, they might well have sported a beard to register that fact. In art, Jesus and many other biblical characters (such as Moses and Abraham) were characteristically portrayed with beards. By the mid-nineteenth century this age-old connection between religion and beard-wearing became accentuated; shaving, in fact, came to be considered unnatural and, therefore, ungodly. There was some discussion that by shaving, the British were displaying narcissistic and immoral tendencies.

Alternatively, your ancestor may have worn a beard for cultural reasons. Jewish men wore beards to show their observance of the Old Testament. Talmudic tradition allows Jewish men to trim their beards with scissors but not with a razor. This is because the action of a single blade against the skin is thought to 'mar' the beard, whereas scissors work by the contact of two blades. Hasidic Jews traditionally do not remove or trim their beards, since Kabbalah (Jewish mysticism) suggests that the beard hairs are channels of subconscious holy energy flowing from above to the human soul.

SHAVING

Of course, your Victorian ancestor's beard probably had as much to do with the availability and efficiency of shaving implements and materials as with any of the concerns mentioned above. While shaving with flint razors has technically been possible since Neolithic times, the business of shaving was long-winded and fraught with frustration until the introduction of straight steel razors (produced in Sheffield) in the late seventeenth century. The blades in these early razors, however, became dull quickly and had to be honed and stropped (sharpened with a leather strap) regularly.

In 1847 the first 'hoe type' razor – in which the blade was perpendicular to the handle – was invented by Englishman William Henson. For many

Barbers' shops, which opened on a Sunday, encountered the wrath of the more religious members of the community. (Beamish, The Living Museum of the North)

working-class men in the Victorian period, having a shave meant going to a barber's shop on their day off – usually a Sunday morning – a time that did not sit well with many in the anti-shaving lobby. Here is how one Victorian commentator, Thomas Wright, described the practice in *Some Habits and Customs of the Working Classes*, published in 1867:

> Sunday morning is always an exceedingly busy time in a barber's shop in a working-class neighbourhood. Many of those who only shave once a week habitually choose Sunday for the operation; others, who usually undergo their weekly shave on Saturday, will sometimes, if they find the shop full when they call on that day, or are themselves very busy, or not going out till dark or something of that kind, defer the shaving till the next morning. Some again, who have been shaved on the Saturday, but who are rather particular about their personal appearance, have another 'scrape' on the Sunday-morning, in order to be 'all of a piece', when dressed in their Sunday clothes; while the swellish-inclined, who have already put on their Sunday suits, and are going out for the day, come to have their hair brushed and 'done up'. Again, numbers of men who do not care about dressing to go for a morning walk, and yet do not wish to be hanging about the house while the cooking operations are going on, take a shave or a brush-up as an excuse for joining in the lively conversation and newsmongering of the barber's shop.

For the first safety razor (with a wire skin guard along the razor's edge) our ancestors had to wait until an invention from the American Kampfe brothers in the 1880s. Even on this model the blade had to be removed often for sharpening. Shaving became much more popular after the invention of the first disposable razor blade by King Camp Gillette (a salesman for the Baltimore Seal Company) in America in 1895. Over the next few years the razor was modified, until it became T-shaped with a double-edged, disposable and replaceable blade. By 1905 these razors were being marketed in Europe. In 1910 the American Willis G. Shockey received an American patent for his wind-up safety razor. This was the forerunner of the electric razor: its wind-up-by-hand flywheel operated for a short period of time.

While your Victorian and Edwardian ancestors may have been gloriously bearded, the chances are that their sons and grandsons from the second decade of the twentieth century onwards were clean-shaven. A growing awareness of the connection between bacteria and health in the Edwardian period also helped to usher in a period of clean-shavenness. During the

First World War, Gillette worked out a deal with the American military that ensured every American soldier had a disposable razor as part of his standard issue gear. All soldiers were required to shave their beards so that gas masks could seal over their faces. While the wearing of beards declined in this period, moustaches flourished, and became a symbol of rank. In general, the younger the man the less extravagant his moustache.

A popular Victorian advert for Pear's shaving stick. (Beamish, The Living Museum of the North)

Facial hair and the tending of it has given rise to a number of artefacts that today frequently turn up in antique shops and sometimes as inherited family items. In the nineteenth and early twentieth centuries moustaches were characteristically kept in trim with wax, nets (snoods), brushes and scissors. The 1860s saw the invention of the 'moustache cup': a drinking cup with a semicircular ledge inside, which acted as a guard to keep the moustache dry.

If you have inherited your ancestor's shaving kit, treasure it. There are few items that will have seen so much use by a forebear. Indeed, if he was clean-shaven and lived to the age of 75, he will probably have used his brush and razor up to 20,000 times. Rumour has it that Queen Victoria laid out Prince Albert's shaving gear every day after his death. Certainly, few artefacts will ever bring you as close to departed loved ones.

FIND OUT MORE

Helen Bunkin and Randall Williams, *Beards, Beards, Beards*, Hunter & Cyr, 2000.

Reginald Reynolds, *Beards: Their Social Standing, Religious Involvements, Decorative Possibilities, and Value in Offence and Defence Through the Ages*, Doubleday, 1949.

Allan Peterkin, *One Thousand Beards. A Cultural History of Facial Hair*, Arsenal Pulp Press, 2001.

www.beards.org – all you ever need to know about growing a beard.

www.quikshave.com/timeline.htm – a timeline of shaving history.

mustachesofthenineteenthcentury.pbwiki.com – specialised terminology for moustaches of the nineteenth century.

5

Marks of Distinction

DISTINGUISHING FEATURES

Distinguishing physical characteristics from facial moles to webbed feet can be a delightful, perturbing and certainly memorable element of the stories of family history. Sadly, perhaps, because of our current society's fascination with achieving physical perfection, a harelip or a lame leg may be the only aspects of our ancestors that we are aware of before we begin properly to research their histories. But references to our ancestors' physical peculiarities need not simply be a matter of tales and hearsay – they often get fully and richly described in all sorts of historical records, including photographs, passports, and criminal, military and hospital records.

Stories and records that flag up physical attributes can do more than help us to picture what an ancestor looked like. For a start, they may remind us of the physical traits that we or our offspring have inherited. The most commonly inherited facial features are dimples in the cheeks, a cleft in the chin, double eyelids, the shape of the nose and the thickness of the lips. Some features may remind us of the ethnic or even regional backgrounds of our ancestors ('Irish eyes', Scottish red hair or Slavic cheekbones, for example). One peculiar deformity of the hands, 'Dupuytren's Contracture' (named after a famous French surgeon), affected many of our north European ancestors, causing an inability to correctly flex the fingers. If you have it, it may mean that you are descended from Viking stock.

While Victorian photographers may have retouched negatives to get rid of facial blemishes, European ladies of the eighteenth century joyfully applied artificial beauty spots to enhance their attraction. (Circle of Francois-Hubert Drouais (1727–75), *Portrait of a Lady*, traditionally identified as Anne de la Grange-Trianon (1632–1707), Countess of Palluau and Frontenac)

More interestingly, perhaps, scars, wounds and other injuries may also sometimes tell us something about our ancestors' experiences, possibly indicating accidents befallen, violence endured or injuries incurred during wartime – all of which may be corroborated by other historical records.

PHOTOGRAPHS

Nowadays, anyone with a scanner and a good image editing programme can improve old photographs by electronically smoothing out creases, scuffs and scratches, correcting fading and discolouration, and removing spots and stains caused by mould, mildew, moisture and water streaking. Photos that have been darkened by age can also be made lighter and brighter. If you are unable to do this yourself, there are plenty of commercial websites that will do it for you. This process in itself might reveal new aspects of your ancestor's physical appearance; even simply scanning a photograph, increasing its size or improving the resolution, can better reveal any unusual features that your ancestor might have had, such as heavy brows, hair with distinctive grey streaking or albinism.

Distinguishing marks on photographs can help identify whether an ancestor in two different images is the same individual. Great-aunt's distinctive widow's peak, for example, might be a give-away detail in a series of photographs long separated in time. However, be careful. Don't assume that the absence of a particular characteristic means that the two pictures are of different individuals. Some distinguishing features can change over time. Moles may appear in middle age that were not present when the subject was younger; scars and birthmarks can disappear with age. In addition, different photographic processes can show up distinguishing marks to varying degrees. A mole or birthmark, for example, might be much darker and more visible in a high-contrast Daguerrotype portrait (most popular in the 1850s) but almost invisible in a low-contrast tintype portrait (popular in the 1860s).

If you know that your ancestor had a particular physical characteristic that isn't apparent from a photograph, be aware that the negatives of many nineteenth-century photographs were retouched to remove or improve any perceived defects or blemishes. Retouching was frowned upon before the 1860s because it interfered with the 'truthfulness' of the image, but thenceforth it was a popular way of enhancing photographs, with the debate among photographers shifting to which techniques might best be used.

Photographers in the past could remove warts, spots and freckles, take away bags under the eyes and double chins, and even change the shape of a figure. Some of this work would be done as a matter of course before the image was presented to the customer. Once proof prints had been issued, the customer could, if necessary, recommend that further retouching be undertaken. Some retouching was done to the negative and may not be obvious now; but retouching work that was undertaken on the surface of the photographic print can be very apparent today. This is because the retouching medium may have aged differently from the print surface.

An American family-history researcher recently sufficiently tidied up a photograph of her great-great-grandmother, Mary Weaver, to see properly for the first time all the lines and wrinkles on her face. This led her to speculate about the difficulties of Mary's life in rural Pennsylvania and the physical effects of some of the traumas she had been through: the births of seven children, the deaths of various family members, and her ejection from the family home by an errant son. For this researcher, the business of cleaning up the family photograph and seeing her ancestor's facial features more clearly really did produce some startling results, and gave her a better understanding of her ancestor's life. Her fascinating article is at www.jamagenee.hubpages. com/hub/Up-Close-and-Personal-With-Dead-Ancestors.

PASSPORTS

The clearest photographs that you will possibly have of an ancestor will be his or her passport image. Luckily for the researcher, evidence from the camera here is often backed up by a written description of the holder's appearance. Old blue passports issued from 1920 to 1988 (when they were superseded by the burgundy EU passport) included a section on physical attributes. The face shape might be described as 'round' or 'oval', the complexion as 'fair', 'dark' or even 'fresh', and the size and shape of some features might also be recorded (forehead: 'broad'; nose: 'flat'; eyes: 'small'; mouth: 'medium'). Passports may also mention beards and moustaches, the shape of the chin (usually 'round' or 'cleft') and the colour of the hair ('dark', 'black' or 'fair'). 'Special peculiarities', such as 'spectacles worn' or 'mole on the right shoulder', might also appear. The recently discovered passport of the author James Joyce (1882–1941) and his family, issued by the British consulate in Zurich in 1915, describes him as 5ft 10in tall, with a 'regular' forehead, nose and mouth, blue eyes, oval chin and dark brown hair. His 'wife' Nora (they were not in fact married until 1931) is described as 5ft 3in tall, with a 'regular' face, nose and mouth, grey eyes, a 'sound' chin and brown hair.

MILITARY RECORDS

Many military service records can be accessed at www.ancestry.co.uk, www.thegenealogist.co.uk and www.findmypast.co.uk. At the time of enlistment and discharge in the First World War height and chest measurements were taken (see chapter 7) and a record was made of eye and hair colour and type of complexion. There was a separate section for 'Descriptive Marks', which could include scars, other injuries, tattoos or birthmarks. Service records may also include medical history forms, casualty forms and disability statements, detailing the appearance and provenance of injuries suffered. Pension records of soldiers who fought in the First World War (also available at www.ancestry.co.uk) also include remarks on injuries incurred, which might have left physical traces in the life yet to come.

The following is part of the transcript of the record of Private Wilfred Wilkinson of the Royal Marine Light Infantry from a database (Great Britain, Royal Naval Division Casualties of the Great War, 1914–1924) available at www.ancestry.co.uk. The abbreviation 'GSW' tucked away under 'Service History' refers to a gunshot wound he incurred in the thigh, some months before he was killed.

Name: Wilfred Wilkinson
Service Branch: Royal Marine Light Infantry
Unit: 1st Royal Marine Bn.
Rank: Private
Death Date: 17 Febr 1917
Cause of Death: Killed in Action
Burial: Queen's Cemetery, Bucquoy (FR514)
Service History: Enlisted 26/7/15; Embarked RM Brigade 16/2/16 (per HMT 'Olympic' and arrived Mudros 24/2/16 to Base Details), joined 1st RM Bn. 25/4/16-13/11/16 GSW thigh and Scabies, rejoined 1st RM Bn 3/12/16-17/2/17 DD
Service Number: PLY/970/S

IMMIGRATION, EMIGRATION AND PASSENGER LISTS

Many of the big family history websites give access to the records of passengers who immigrated to the New World or travelled there for business or pleasure, as well as of ancestors who immigrated to the UK. The amount of information collected on each passenger depends greatly on when exactly he or she travelled and which port he or she left from or arrived at, but sometimes physical characteristics (including 'Marks of Identification') are recorded. One interesting example of this is miners who travelled *en masse* to America from Lancashire in the Edwardian period. The passenger lists reveal that they manifested all manner of injuries from crooked jaws to missing fingers – many of which must have been occupational injuries.

TRANSPORTATION AND OTHER CRIMINAL RECORDS

Large numbers of criminals who could not be fitted into Britain's overcrowded prisons were transported to Australia from 1787 onwards. They were often fully described in ships' records – indeed, those doing the recording seemed to relish creating detailed physical accounts of their motley human cargo. A large collection of such records, some of which include descriptions of physical characteristics, can be searched at the Australian Convict Collection at www.ancestry.co.uk. Similar records may be searched at www.convictcentral.com.

On the convict ship *Pyrenees* (which arrived in Western Australia in 1851), for example, there were a number of distinctive-looking individuals sporting numerous 'marks of punishment', scars and broken teeth. One such was John Aspernal, a cotton spinner of 5ft 7⅛in, whose description began well with 'light brown hair, blue eyes and an oval face'. Further details prove, however, that he was by no means an attractive physical specimen. Indeed, he was 'rather stout' with 'a face heavily pitted by smallpox', 'very bald and with three teeth missing on his right jaw'. Thomas Johnson, a labourer who travelled on the *Vimeira* in 1865, was 5ft 1½in tall, stout with dark brown hair, grey eyes, a round face and fresh complexion; but he had a cast in his left eye and the third finger of his left hand was bruised. Other distinguishing features recorded were freckles, 'pock pit' marks, lumps, scars and cuts, broken noses, missing digits, and limbs contracted from burns. Details of the crimes committed by these men, including rape, robbery with violence and assault, may go some way to explaining some of their injuries.

Various other kinds of record relating to those with criminal convictions may include physical descriptions. The 4,400 licences for parole for female convicts (1853–71 and 1883–87), for example, which may be viewed online at www.ancestry.co.uk, include 550 mugshots of female prisoners together with documents that may include written descriptions of physical appearance. Other documents that may record the same sort of information are the court orders recording prisoners' movements from prison to prison (1842–71), available to view at the National Archives, Kew.

HOSPITAL RECORDS

If your ancestor incurred a disfiguring injury or even just a broken arm or leg, you may be able to find out more from his or her hospital records.

A family history researcher remembered that his grandfather, John Williams (b.1894), had been afflicted by a withered right arm. He could not remember ever being told whether this was a deformity from birth or an injury incurred later in life. Hospital records for the Evelina Children's Hospital in London (www.hharp.org.uk) solved the mystery. At the age of 4 in April 1898, the unfortunate boy had been admitted for treatment because he was suffering from 'scalds to his chest and right arm'. The records showed that he was in hospital for thirty-eight days, and the reason given for his admittance was 'violence'. This is a grim and dramatic example of how investigating the distinguishing feature of an ancestor may help you to discover more about his or her life experiences and family circumstances.

Before the arrival of the NHS in 1948 (when a comprehensive, universal system was introduced), the British hospital system was a hotchpotch of state-run and voluntary institutions. Where and how you were treated depended very much on where you lived, what sort of medical problems you had and, at times, on how wealthy you were.

Hospital records, including admission registers and casebooks, have been around for centuries, but in the Victorian period the pressure on hospital managers to keep better and more accurate records was greater. Many hospitals had charitable status, and those in charge were required to produce annual statistics and reports to show that donated money was being wisely

Hospital records, available at www.hharp.org, may point to ailments and conditions suffered by your ancestor. These case notes refer to John Pretlove, a 10-month-old child from Winchmore Hill, Middlesex, who was admitted to Great Ormond Street Hospital on 24 February 1911 suffering from bronchitis and – notably – a cleft palate. He had an operation, which improved the situation, and was released sixteen days later. (www.hharp. org, Historic Hospital Admission Records Project)

spent. The keeping of patient records helped them to do just this. Casebooks were kept by doctors themselves, and served as a record of how they had treated patients.

The records of a small number of hospitals in London and Glasgow (mainly dealing with children) are now available online at the website of the Historic Hospital Admission Records Project (HHARP), www.hharp.org.uk. This is a joint venture between Kingston University and several archives holding records for children's hospitals. The database covers the records of the Hospital for Sick Children at Great Ormond Street (1852–1914), its convalescent home Cromwell House (1869–1910), the Evelina Hospital (1874–77 and 1889–1902), the Alexandra Hospital for Children with Hip Disease (1867–95) and the Glasgow Royal Hospital for Sick Children (Yorkhill) (1883–1903).

Depending on which of these hospitals your ancestor was admitted to, you may find out a variety of information about him or her, including dates of admission, year of birth, age on admission (in years and months), thumbnails of handwritten case notes (in a small number of cases), residence details, name of doctor, ward, length of stay, what your ancestor was admitted for, the outcome of the hospital stay (whether or not he or she was relieved, whether or not he or she died), date of discharge, where he or she was discharged to, his or her infantile disease and vaccination history, and even post-mortem results.

For the records of hospitals not on the HHARP database, check to see if the hospital has its own archives, as in the case of some of the bigger and older hospitals, such as St Bartholomew's (London) and Addenbrooke's (Cambridge). The location of the records of 2,800 other hospitals can be searched via the Hospital Records Database (a joint project between the National Archives and the Wellcome Library) on the National Archives website (www.nationalarchives.gov.uk/hospitalrecords/). The database lists the records available for each hospital, their covering dates and the archive holding them. Similar information regarding the records of voluntary hospitals can also be obtained by searching the voluntary hospitals database (www.hospitalsdatabase.lshtm.ac.uk), kept by the London School of Hygiene and Tropical Medicine. Information about the records of Scottish hospitals (their type and the location of the archives which keep them) can be searched at www.clinicalnotes.ac.uk.

Before making any visit to view hospital archives, do check carefully. By no means all hospital records include the patient details and case notes that are so interesting to family historians.

SOME INTERESTING EXAMPLES

The list of distinguishing features that your ancestor might have displayed is long and varied, but here is a detailed look at some of the most interesting types:

LEFT-HANDEDNESS

Left-handedness tends to run in families, although how exactly it is passed down remains a mystery. From the mid-nineteenth century onwards our ancestors might well have suffered social disapprobation if they showed any sign of this particular physical characteristic. Victorian anthropologists found

Premier Institut Médical

de

Beauté, Maladies de la Peau et du Cuir Chevelu

DIRIGÉ PAR

le Dr. LEONE FRIEDMANN

Membre de la Société de Dermatologie et Syphiligraphie de Paris.
Ancien assistant à la clinique de Maladies de la Peau et syphilitiques des Universités de Berlin et de Florence.
Ancien assistant du professeur Golgi, lauréat du prix international Nobel.

București. — Strada Franclin, No. 14. — București

CONSULTATIONS DE 10 à 12 et 2 à 5

Guérison sans douleur de: la chute des cheveux, des taches de la figure, même celles de naissance, des boutons, des taches de rousseur, du nez rouge, des points noirs. Enlèvement des cicatrices, des naevi (verrues) et des poils superflus du visage (épilation).

Correction des nez difformes (aplatis, déviés etc.), sans opérations et sans douleur.

Guérison du *lupus* par les rayons ultra-violets d'après la méthode du Professeur Finsen.

Installation la plus moderne pour la guérison radicale des maladies de la peau, vénériennes et syphilitiques.

Prix modestes à la portée de tous. Informations et prospectus illustrés gratis sur demande.

Few of our ancestors could probably have afforded the treatments available at this beauty centre in Bucharest in 1911. Among other services, it offered the 'pain-free treatment of acne, alopecia, birthmarks, blackheads, port-wine stains and rosacea; the removal of scars or moles; depilation; and the non-surgical correction of deformed noses'. (Tout-Bucarest, *Almanach du High Life de l'Indépendance Roumaine*, 1911. An item held in the DacoRomanica archive, Bucharest City Library) that there was a greater than usual incident of left-handedness in so-called primitive tribes such as the Bushmen and the Hottentots. They also concluded that much primitive art had been made with the left hand. From this, they erroneously came to the conclusion that right-handedness was a sign of the greater civilisation of British culture, and that left-handedness was an inadequacy that needed to be stamped out.

The social stigma against left-handedness in Victorian England led to school children being forced to write with their right hands, sometimes having their left hand forcibly tied behind their back to this end. Victorian writer Charles Dodgson, better known as Lewis Carroll (1832–98), was a left-hander who demonstrated other characteristics often related to left-handedness, including stammering, emotionality and a tendency to reclusiveness. His fascination with his own 'sinister' tendencies was most brilliantly demonstrated in *Alice Through the Looking Glass* (1871), in which the heroine steps through the mirror on her mantelpiece into an inverted world where left has become right.

Left-handedness came to be associated with all manner of psychiatric disorders. The 'Jack the Ripper' murders of the late 1880s were believed to have been carried out by a left-hander, since the throats of some of the victims were slashed from left to right. John Netley, a left-handed London cab driver, was at one point suspected of the crimes. Much was made of the fact that Netley had been an identical twin: there is a greater than usual incidence of left-handedness among such twins. The Italian criminologist Cesare Lombroso (1835–1909) defined a theory of criminal anthropology which held that deviance was a matter of inheritance, and he used all manner of bodily evidence (including physiognomy and other physical defects) to prove this. As a result, left-handedness in the Edwardian period became strongly associated with degeneracy and crime. Before long the eugenics movement took up the cause of right-handedness, and being left-handed became synonymous with both limited mental ability and moral degeneracy.

BIRTHMARKS

Birthmarks may be inherited but more commonly are not. Your ancestor's birthmarks may have been vascular (red, blue or purple): strawberry marks, portwine stains, hemangiomas and salmon patch (stork marks); or pigmented (brown): 'café au lait spots' or Mongolian birthmarks. Distinctive birthmarks, such as those shaped like maps, rabbits or other unusual phenomena, are often the subject of family anecdotes which seek to explain how they might have been obtained. They range from what a mother might have eaten while she was pregnant to an accident she may have had, or something she may have seen. Needless to say, all of these old wives' tales are untrue!

MOLES AND BEAUTY SPOTS

Such are the vagaries of fashion that in the eighteenth century wealthy women occasionally applied false moles to their faces as marks of beauty; sometimes these were in attractive shapes, such as hearts or stars made from velvet. By the nineteenth century, by contrast, such marks on the face were generally regarded as ugly and indicative of bad luck, lechery (if they appeared on a man's nose) or sexual promiscuity (if they appeared on a woman's thigh). Moles on the face, especially the chin and neck, could indicate wealth, and on the chest and stomach, strength. Real moles are caused by an excess of pigmentation in certain areas of the body. Some may be inherited; thus, theoretically, you could have a mole in exactly the same place that your ancestor had one (the phenomenon may skip a generation or two). This is apparently even more likely in the case of people with many moles. In certain cases around the world the reappearance of a family mole on the body of a member of the younger generation has been superstitiously attributed to the reincarnation of an ancestor.

CLEFT CHIN

Cleft chins are an inherited characteristic resulting from an incomplete fusion of the left and right parts of the jaw bone or jaw muscle. At large genealogical reunions it is often the recurrence of the shape of a chin across many branches of a family that most delights the people attending. It is possible that such a trait might indicate that your distant ancestors hailed from other shores. Cleft chins occur all over the world but are particularly common in people of Germanic or West Slavic origin.

WIDOW'S PEAK

A V-shaped point in the hairline at the centre of the forehead (similar to the shape of a traditional widow's cap) is an inherited trait that often occurs in tandem with eyes that are widely spaced. People with widow's peaks have characteristically been stigmatised as stern, peculiar or even evil. It was traditionally believed that women with such a distinctive feature would become widows early.

All these examples show that certain distinguishing characteristics are inherited, many are the subject of folklore, some belie ancestry from other places and ethnicities, and yet others follow the vagaries of fashion. The examples here are meant to whet your appetite. Whatever your ancestor's particular physical peculiarities, the Internet can provide a wealth of fascinating detail and material for speculation.

FIND OUT MORE

Jennifer Boothroyd, *Facial Features: Freckles, Earlobes, Noses and More*, Lerner Publications, 2012.

Bill Cordingley, *In Your Face: What Facial Features Reveal about the People You Know and Love*, New Horizon Press, 2001.

David T. Hawkings, *Criminal Ancestors*, Stroud, 1996.

Robert Hughes, *The Fatal Shore: History of the Transportation of Convicts to Australia, 1787–1868*, Harvill Press, 1996.

www.birthmarks.com – listing many superstitions about the acquisition and meaning of birthmarks.

www.convictcentral.com – convict records to Australia.

www.hharp.org – Historic Hospital Admission Records Project.

6

Inked

TATTOOS

*D*ragons and dolphins, wreaths and rose briars, threaded through with a curious notation of names and dates, are today the stuff of tattoos sported by everyone, it seems, from film celebrities to teenage girls. But self-decoration of this kind is not a modern phenomenon and, strange as it may seem, tattooing has been a significant, if bizarre, way of registering identity for a couple of hundred years.

A family history researcher was recently investigating an ancestor who was a conductor on the Manchester trams in the early years of the twentieth century. She knew little about him apart from the fact that he had died in his forties; no living member of her family recalled him and she had no photographs. Thus she was thrilled to discover from his military records (accessed through www.ancestry.co.uk) that he sported a tattoo of a ballerina on his right forearm! Suddenly this mysterious relative came to life. What sort of man would champion such an image? Was the ballerina a girlfriend, a wife or just a fantasy? Was the tattoo a carefully considered tribute to a relationship, or a terrible mistake acquired during a moment of madness?

Working out why your ancestor chose to have a tattoo, will be a matter of guesswork, because tattoos have always had many possible meanings. The earliest may even have been used for medicinal purposes – to cure arthritis in the joints, for example. Later, tattoos were used to convey ideas of status, belonging, patriotism, achievement or conquest. Sometimes they recognised a relationship or an important date. Occasionally they paid tribute to a type of employment, interest or hobby. Additionally they might have provided sexual titillation, or registered a protest against someone or something.

The size, shape, colouring and site of tattoos throughout history was, of course, largely a matter of individual choice, but as the craft developed some designs became standard and could be customised according to the client's needs. If you become aware (from a written record or photographs) that your ancestor had tattoos, you may be able to find the actual design and its possible significance. The level of detail given by the historical record can be crucial. Heart tattoos with banners including the name of a loved one were very popular with First World War soldiers, for example, but there were also hands holding hearts (a symbol of paternal love), black hearts (a symbol of mourning) and golden hearts (a symbol of 'a consciousness of God'). Speculate on the possible meanings of your ancestors' tattoos by consulting one of the books or websites on vintage tattoos mentioned in the Find Out More section at the end of the chapter.

TATTOOS: A BRIEF HISTORY

Tattooing has an ancient heritage in many cultures, including North European ones. After disappearing from our shores for many centuries, however, the art was rediscovered and reintroduced after explorers visited distant parts of the world where it was practised in the sixteenth, seventeenth and eighteenth centuries. European sailors started to acquire tattoos after Captain James Cook sailed the South Pacific and arrived on the island of Tahiti in 1768. Intrigued by the local practice of body painting (the word 'tattoo' is probably derived from the Tahitian word *tatau*), many of the sailors, including Cook's science officer and expedition botanist, Sir James Banks, obtained their own tattoos. Once back in Britain, the sailors showed off their distinctive inkings, and a new craze was born.

In the early days tattooing in Britain was done by hand using a needle. Ink was then rubbed into the wound. Tattoos were popular among working men (and women) from the late eighteenth century onwards, but the practice was at first confined to a few parlours in seaside ports. In the last decades of the nineteenth century, however, tattooing became surprisingly upmarket, appealing even to members of the British Royal Family and the aristocracy. In 1891 an electric tattooing machine (based on Edison's electric pen) was patented by American Samuel O'Reilly, and soon adopted on this

The butterfly tattoo of miner Billy Longstaff of Sherburn Hill Colliery, Durham, is in stark and poignant contrast to his tough life underground in the 1950s. (Gilesgate Archives and Beamish, The Living Museum of the North)

side of the Atlantic. The electric machine meant that body decoration could now be obtained at a reasonable price. As tattoos came once more within the budget of more of our ordinary ancestors, tattoos started to lose their appeal for the upper classes.

SAILORS AND TATTOOS

Nautical men are the most likely of our ancestors to have had tattoos. Some sailors opted for simple designs, popularly their own name or initials, or the names of family and friends; others flaunted the names of places visited around the world. Some tattoos signalled a specific job role. A dock worker, for example, might be decorated with a rope around the forearm; a member of the fishing fleet might sport a harpoon; guns or crossed cannon indicated military naval service. Some common tattoos adopted by many sailors promised to guarantee good fortune in what was a very hazardous career. Two stars, for example, suggested that the bearer might always find his way to his desired destination. A rooster and a pig decorating the calves or feet were thought to ensure safety at sea, probably because these animals (travelling as they did in lightweight wooden crates) often survived shipwrecks. Other tattoos may tell you more about your sailor ancestor's individual career at sea: sailing 5,000 nautical miles (a swallow); sailing the Atlantic (an anchor); crossing the equator (a turtle standing on its back legs, or King Neptune); sailing around Cape Horn (a full-rigged ship often across the whole back); sailing into the port of China (a dragon); or crossing the international dateline (a golden dragon).

Other nautical tattoos were more intricate, and may have signified a prevailing maxim by which a life was lived. A man carrying an anchor, for instance, stood for 'I carry all my hopes with me'; and a woman holding scales and an anchor for 'I have hope in justice'.

CONVICTS, TRANSPORTATION AND TATTOOS

Richly described in ships' records, nineteenth-century convict ancestors who were transported to the penal colonies of Australia often sported tattoos. Common designs included suns, stars, mermaids, fish, flowerpots and bugles. Ex-labourer Edward Byrne, for example, was a convict on the *Phoebe Dunbar*, which travelled from Kingstown in Ireland to Swan River Colony, Western Australia in 1853. According to the ship's records (available to view at www.convictcentral.com), he bore a tattoo of the letter 'E' on his left arm and 'EP' (possibly a mistake in transcription for his initials 'EB') on his right arm. Another convict aboard the same ship, James Casey, bore an ink ring on the second finger of both his right and left hands and an anchor on his back. Fellow convict Michael Doyle was more gloriously decorated still, with the word 'SWEEP' and two anchors on his right arm, 'a laurel, a tree and a star on his right band [sic]', 'an anchor on his left arm' and 'a cross on the back of his left hand'. Other convict tattoos may have been badges of honour – some criminal gangs in London insisted on tattooing as a mark of belonging – and the rings inked on the fingers of some convicts may have been an indication of real or *de facto* marriages.

MILITARY MEN AND TATTOOS

Tattooing in the British military has had a mixed history. The age-old practice of branding criminals with a hot or cold iron was made obsolete in 1829, but in the mid-nineteenth century badly behaved soldiers were still being tattooed (using ink or gunpowder) with a D' for 'Deserter' or 'BC' for 'Bad Character'. From 1851 regulations were tightened up, and the tattooing of soldiers had to be carried out by a regimental surgeon rather than by a drum major or bugle major, as had originally been the case. The British Mutiny Act of 1858 stipulated that deserters be marked on the left side 2in below the armpit with a letter 'D', not less than 1in long.

Ironically, just as tattooing as military punishment was being outlawed in Britain (in 1879), other sorts of tattoo were becoming very popular. With British troops required on all fronts to defend the Empire, Field Marshal Earl Roberts (1832–1914), himself tattooed, suggested that every officer should be inked with his regimental crest. Such decoration would not only improve morale among men far from home, he argued, but could also be crucial in helping to identify casualties on foreign battlefields. The famous London tattooist Tom Riley started his business after honing his skills on soldiers in the South African (Second Boer) War (1899–1902) and the Sudan Campaigns (1881–98), and his fellow tattooist Sutherland Macdonald practised tattooing while serving in the Royal Engineers. By the start of the First World War many ordinary men joining the forces had already acquired tattoos – usually of a playful rather than a regimental kind – in their leisure time, and others acquired them out of camaraderie as the war progressed.

To find out whether or not your military ancestors were tattooed when they joined up, take a look at their service records on either www.ancestry.co.uk (Military Records) or www.findmypast.co.uk (Armed Forces and Conflict Records). The records held on each soldier vary, but if the second page of the enlistment papers is available look for the section on 'Distinctive Marks'. Here, tattoos were mentioned alongside moles, birthmarks and other defining physical features. Medical history forms and discharge papers might also mention tattoos.

Enlistment record of Evan Edward Smith, Merthyr Tydfil, 4 November, 1907. His tattoos include a large cross with the words 'In Memory of My Dear Mother' (suggesting his mother is dead), clasped hands over a heart (indicating paternal love) and anchors (indicating his naval career). (www.findmypast.co.uk)

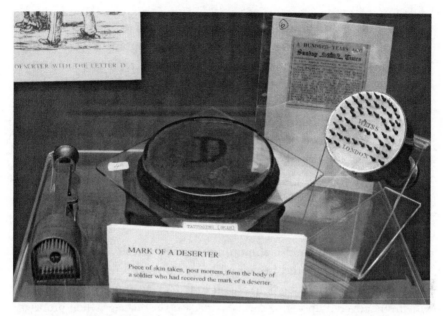

This exhibit at the Army Medical Services Museum, Hampshire, features a tattooed piece of skin taken post-mortem from a British army deserter, together with the equipment used to do the branding. (Photographed by Gaius Cornelius)

THE ARISTOCRACY AND TATTOOS

From the mid-nineteenth century onwards tattoos came to be considered exotic and lavish fashion items. The fad was even endorsed by royalty; in 1862 the Prince of Wales, later Edward VII, visited the Holy Land and had a small tattoo of the Jerusalem Cross tattooed on his arm. Twenty years later his two sons, the Duke of Clarence and the Duke of York (later George V) travelled to Japan and acquired dragon tattoos (etched by the master tattooist Hori Chiro).

The passion for tattoos among the British aristocracy caused consternation among the Japanese authorities, who thought the practice old-fashioned and barbaric. Nevertheless, artistic tattoos acquired in Japan (known as *irezumi*) were very popular in British high society in the 1890s. By 1898 there were also about twenty tattoo artists at work in London, including the masters of the art: Tom Riley (The Strand), Sutherland MacDonald (Jermyn Street), and brothers George Burchett (Davis) and Charles Davis (Waterloo Road). Favourite designs for aristocrats were family crests, birds, serpents, flowers and plants. Army officers demanded regimental logos, and sportsmen asked for inspirational images such as running horses. Thomas Lipton (1848–1931), the famous British tea merchant, reputedly had a tattoo of a sailing ship across his chest.

By 1895 some Members of Parliament were sporting tattoos of initials, family crests and shields. Lord Charles Beresford (1846–1919), a British admiral and member of parliament, is rumoured to have had a large tattoo of a fox-hunting scene tattooed on his back (or, in some accounts, on his buttocks!). And the craze for tattoos among the rich and powerful continued long into the twentieth century, with even the Norwegian king, Haakon VII, getting a tattoo during his exile in London during the Second World War.

Aristocratic women also sometimes sported tattoos. Lady Randolph Churchill (1854–1921), the mother of Prime Minister Winston Churchill, is said to have had an etching of a serpent in red, green and blue on her wrist, which she covered up with a specially made silver bracelet when propriety so decreed, while the eccentric Princess Marie of Denmark (1865–1909) had a tattoo of an anchor inked on her arm.

TATTOOS AND THE CIRCUS

Every major circus in the nineteenth and early twentieth centuries employed several heavily tattooed people, some as sideshow attractions and others as circus performers such as jugglers and sword swallowers. In America the tattooed lady was a regular sight in the circus. In addition to their visual peculiarities, these highly painted characters provided entertainment by telling gripping tales of having been captured by savages and tattooed against their will. Some of our ancestors may have obtained their tattoos from artists who practised and exhibited at travelling circuses during the spring and summer before returning to their urban studios in the winter.

TATTOOING IN CONCENTRATION CAMPS

Unfortunately, some of our ancestors' tattoos may have had a far more sinister heritage. Prisoners including Jews, gypsies and other 'undesirables' arriving at the Auschwitz concentration camp complex during the Second

World War were branded with serial numbers by the SS authorities from the autumn of 1941 onwards. Initially the numbers were made across the upper left chest using a special metal stamp with interchangeable numbers comprising 1cm-long needles. The number was punched at one blow and indelible ink was then rubbed into the wound. Later, a single needle was used and the number was tattooed on to the outer side of the left forearm; some prisoners had numbers tattooed on the inner side of the left forearm. Those people sent directly to the gas chambers were not registered or given serial numbers.

If the message boards of genealogical websites are anything to go by, tattoos are a source of much fascination and speculation among family historians across the world. Such sites are awash with people searching for information about ancestors and current missing relatives who might be identified by their distinctive body decoration. Never rule out any ancestor from having had a tattoo. Lady Steel (wife of the former Liberal Democrat leader Lord Steel) has, for example, recently confessed to treating herself to a tattoo of a pink jaguar – part of her husband's coat of arms – on her shoulder, to celebrate her seventieth birthday!

FIND OUT MORE

James Bradley et al, *Written on the Body: The Tattoo in European and American History*, Reaktion Books, 2000.

Carol Clerk, *Vintage Tattoos*, Carlton Books, 2011.

Steven G. Gilbert, *Tattoo History: A Sourcebook*, Juno Books, 2000.

Tarisa Green, *The Tattoo Encyclopedia*, Simon and Schuster, 2003.

Margot Mifflin, *Bodies of Subversion: A Secret History of Women and Tattoo*, Juno Publishing, 2001.

Jack Tressider, *The Complete Dictionary of Symbols*, Duncan Baird, 2004.

www.tattooarchive.com/tattoo_history/burchett_george_charles.html – on the tattoo artists George Burchett and Charles Davis.

www.tattoo.co.uk/bthm.htm – British Tattoo History Museum.

www.tattoomuseum.co.uk – Liverpool Tattoo Museum.

www.ushmm.org/wlc/en/article.php?ModuleId=10007056 – Tattoos and numbers: the practice of identifying prisoners at Auschwitz.

www.vanishingtattoo.com – includes an index of hundreds of common contemporary and historical tattoo designs with their meanings.

7

Head and Shoulders Above the Rest

STATURE

Considerations of the height, weight and general stature of our ancestors are never far from the mind when we are looking at photographs from the nineteenth and early twentieth centuries. You may be tall and slim like your grandfather or shorter and plumper than average like those on your mother's side. Given our current century's obsession with the way we look, it is interesting to speculate on how an ancestor's stature may have affected his or her personal history.

In Britain today, the average height of a man is 5ft 9in and of a woman 5ft 4.4in. Just over 100 years ago our ancestors were a little shorter. According to *The Sunlight Year Book* of 1899 (Lever Brothers), the average Englishman was 5ft 7.36in, Scotsman 5ft 8.61in, Irishman 5ft 7.90in and Welshman 5ft 6.66in. The average height of women in England in 1899 was 5ft 2.65in.

Finding out about your ancestor's vital statistics can be tricky. Photographs can give some indication of height. Often in images of couples, a tall man will be pictured seated while his wife stands beside him. This was done so that the two heads could be brought into the same field of focus. Occasionally the roles were reversed if the woman was appreciably the taller.

Rarely, people recorded details of their height and other measurements in diaries or other personal papers. A Lancashire miner, Jack Daniels, wrote the following list in his diary entry for 10 August 1930, when he was 30:

THE FAREWELL.

Victorian men's clothes typically had little ornamentation and consisted of long, skinny trousers and a hat to make them look taller. (*The Girl's Own Paper*, 1888)

Height – 5 ft 4½ inches

Neck – 15 inches

Chest – 37 inches

Chest expanded – 40 inches

Forearm – 11½ inches

Bicep – 11 inches

Bicep expanded – 12½ inches

Waist – 31 inches

Thigh – 19½ inches

Calf – 13½ inches

Wrist – 6⅞ inches

A short but very strong man, Jack's party trick later in life was to lift two 56lb bags of coal above his head. He had not written down the details of his physical size idly: he had been requested to do so by a colliery doctor, who believed him to have the ideal physique for a miner. Jack's stature was an important part of his employability: he had a body that would have equipped him very well for arduous work underground.

Another source of information about stature can be sociological accounts of certain kinds of people in the past. If your ancestors worked in a particular occupation, there may well be accounts of how their kind looked. George Orwell's *The Road to Wigan Pier* (1933), for example, described in splendid detail the usual stature of Lancashire miners:

> They really do look like iron hammered iron statues ... Most of them are small (big men are at a disadvantage in that job) but nearly all of them have the most noble bodies; wide shoulders tapering to slender supple waists, and small pronounced buttocks and sinewy thighs, with not an ounce of waste flesh anywhere ... You can hardly tell by the look of them whether they are young or old. They may be any age up to sixty or even sixty-five, but when they are black and naked they all look alike. No one could do their work who had not a young man's body, and a figure fit for a guardsman at that, just a few pounds of extra flesh on the waist-line, and the constant bending would be impossible.

Inherited clothing, from hats and gloves to longer garments, can be helpful in working out the size of a particular individual. It has been estimated, for instance, that the Victorian writer Charlotte Brontë was only about 5ft tall from the size of her dresses and shoes. Occasionally, a monumental inscription will give an indication of prodigious size, as in the surely exaggerated case of John Middleton, whose epitaph at Hale on the Runcorn to Liverpool road reads: 'Here lyeth the bodye of John Middleton, the Childe – nine feet three. Born 1578 – Dyde 1623.'

Historians have also drawn conclusions about the height of populations in the past by looking at such material evidence as suits of armour, the heights of doorways and coffin sizes. Emily Brontë's height has been estimated at 5ft 6in because her coffin measured 5ft 7in. Clothes from the past have often been used as a method of gauging the average vital statistics of populations, but it is worthwhile remembering that those items which have been preserved (in museums, National Trust properties and the like) are probably the smallest and daintiest (because the most attractive) garments and, therefore, not necessarily representative of the size of the population at large.

There are a number of other ways to discover something about your ancestor's stature. Over the past couple of hundred years plenty of official documentation has required measurements to be recorded, which has included the sorts of military service records, passports, prison records, and medical records mentioned in earlier chapters.

HEIGHT

Though we might like to suppose that our own height is dependent on factors inherited from our ancestors, genetics have actually played a minimal part in height differentials. Height in history has been far more dependent on what people did for a living, where they lived and what culture they came from. Nutritional disparities brought about by differences in the environment in which our ancestors lived have been a key factor; most important of all has been the amount of animal protein (in milk, red meat and fish) that they ate. Other factors influencing height would have been our ancestors' access to healthcare and the welfare state, and their immunity to infection. Inevitably, of course, height differences have also been linked to class status. Our poor urban ancestors were always shorter on average than those who lived as rural aristocrats.

Far more research has been undertaken on the height of men than of women in the past because of the availability of data from military conscripts. By the second half of the nineteenth century elaborate systems for recruiting military personnel, including the recording of their physical condition, were laid down. Since most men entering the military were from the working classes (who made up over 80 per cent of the population), their data has confidently been used to draw conclusions about the height of the general population.

Historians now agree that between the mid-eighteenth century and the second quarter of the nineteenth century (the period of the Industrial Revolution), the average height of British working-class men increased. When Queen Victoria came to the throne, Scotsmen in urban counties were taller than Englishmen in provincial towns, and both of these types were taller than Londoners. These differences were probably due to environmental factors, especially nutrition. While the Scots were poor, they had a highly nourishing diet of pulses, oats and dairy products. Londoners, on the other hand, suffered urban disamenities, disease, unemployment and a high cost of living, all of which played a part in poor health and attendant shortness of stature.

As industrial cities grew towards the middle of the nineteenth century, there was a popular belief – backed up by statistics – that the health and the average height of the population was falling. There was a downswing in the average height of British men in all urban areas, with evidence to suggest that people in the regional cities were taking on some of the problems that London had long suffered.

The end of the nineteenth century witnessed a climb back in average height, and by the time of the First World War it had reached its previous peak. In 1899 the range of heights of most Englishmen was between 5ft 3in and 5ft 9in, with those under or over those heights being considered unusual. The overall growth in height in this period was probably due to a rise in wages, and improvements in public health, quantity and quality of food – all of which led to humans being better able to withstand water-borne and respiratory diseases.

In the latter decades of the nineteenth century officers attending the military training academy at Sandhurst were known to be the tallest military men in the world. The prominence of lofty soldiers – many of them emanating from the upper classes, who traditionally bore tall sons – meant that at the beginning of the First World War the height requirement for the army was optimistically set at 5ft 8in. During the war, however, enlistment standards on height had to change to ensure that enough men might be recruited. You may find your ancestors' enlistment records at www.ancestry.co.uk or www.findmypast.co.uk. The Descriptive Report on Enlistment is the second page of the enlistment papers.

In November 1915 the height requirement for enlistment was reduced to 5ft 3in. But with the high casualty rates, even this new requirement was soon considered to be a limitation. Alfred Bigland, MP for Birkenhead, pressed the War Office in 1914 for permission to form a 'bantam' battalion of men who failed to reach the British Army's normal height requirement but were otherwise perfectly capable of serving. About 3,000 men – many of them previously rejected – rushed to volunteer. These first bantams were formed into the 1st and 2nd Birkenhead battalions of the Cheshire Regiment (later re-designated the 15th and 16th battalions). Bantams had to be not less than 5ft tall and no more than 5ft 3in.

Other regiments that took on bantam divisions were the 20th Battalion of the Lancashire Fusiliers, the West Yorkshire Regiment, the Royal Scots and the Highland Light Infantry. Many bantam recruits were miners. By the end of 1916, however, the general fitness and condition of men volunteering as bantams was no longer up to the standard required, and brigades were informed that no more undersized men would be accepted.

In general terms in Britain, there was continued but slow growth in height in men and women between the two world wars, and then an acceleration in height after the Second World War.

WEIGHT

The weight of people in the past is very hard to ascertain. Very few of our ancestors bothered to record their weight at any point in their lives, still less to chart its rise or fall over a period of time. Some diarists in the past liked to record what they ate; an example of this is George Scotcher, a travelling actor, whose diaries from 1796 to 1800 are in the Victoria and Albert Library. However, few people bothered to link this information to their own body image in any meaningful way.

Only the prodigious in size had their measurements permanently recorded for posterity. This was the case with Daniel Lambert, once the largest man in Britain, who died in 1809 and had this epitaph engraved upon his tombstone:

IN REMEMBRANCE OF THAT PRODIGY IN NATURE.

DANIEL LAMBERT.

A NATIVE OF LEICESTER:

WHO WAS POSSESSED OF AN EXALTED AND CONVIVIAL MIND

AND IN PERSONAL GREATNESS HAD NO COMPETITOR

HE MEASURED THREE FEET ONE INCH ROUND THE LEG

NINE FEET FOUR INCHES ROUND THE BODY

AND WEIGHED

FIFTY TWO STONE ELEVEN POUNDS!

HE DEPARTED THIS LIFE ON THE 21ST OF JUNE 1809

AGED 39 YEARS

An advice book on diet written by Dr A. W. Moore, a member of the Royal College of Surgeons, entitled *Corpulency; ie Fat or Embonpoint in Excess* (1856), included at its end some thirty pages of a 'diet diary'. This was laid out in columns and sections according to days and times of day at which particular foods were eaten. At the end of each day you could record your weight. But this is a rare example of such a record so devoted to recording personal weight in the past – and no copies of this book have been found filled in.

From 1770 the spring scale, invented by Richard Salter, was being used to weigh objects. By the late eighteenth century some shops had large hanging scales upon which customers could weigh themselves. The records of Berry Bros and Rudd in London record that the poet Lord Byron (1788–1824), who was plagued by a fear of becoming obese, went there to be weighed several times. In 1806 (at 18 years old) he was 13st 12lb; five years later he was just 9st.

Other information about diet and weight occasionally turns up in family correspondence or hospital records. Letters between women suggest special diets to be eaten during pregnancy, with which to feed children or tempt the sick, for example, and charts of special diets occasionally turn up among hospital records. Diet reports for British Prime Minister Benjamin Disraeli (1804–81) from the time of his last illness in 1881 are kept at the Royal College of Physicians.

Few working-class Victorians were overweight, because of the hard physical nature of their lives – which required them to walk more, lift more and generally move around more of the time. It is estimated that the average person needed to consume twice the calories we do now just to get through their daily chores. The diet of the lower classes in the early nineteenth century was also notoriously bad. Many existed off little more than bread, butter, potatoes, beer and tea, with the odd slice of bacon thrown in here and there. Many working people had never tasted meat. Others had only eaten 'bad meat', such as tripe, slink (prematurely born calves) or broxy (diseased sheep). Most working-class families did not have ovens before the 1850s, and either ate cold food or food that had been heated in a pan over an open fire. It was only in the last quarter of the nineteenth century that food costs came down: a basket of ordinary household foodstuffs was 30 per cent less expensive in 1889 than it had been in 1877. With the availability of a wider variety of foodstuffs diet improved, and with it fears about overeating.

GREAT BRITAIN.   UNITED STATES.   FRANCE.   GERMANY.   BELGIUM.   RUSSIA.

By the end of the nineteenth century, the British working-class man (pictured here on the extreme left) was considered to be in a superior position to his brothers in the United States, France, Germany, Belgium and Russia – but this cartoon perhaps says more about his economic position than his real physical stature. (*Sunlight Year Book for 1898*)

Among certain sections of the community, however, obesity was definitely a recognised social problem from the mid-nineteenth century. Many prosperous middle- and upper-class Victorian men overindulged on sugar, meats and desserts, and were overweight, unfit and desirous of doing something about it. Many diets were instituted towards the end of the nineteenth century, most famously that of the undertaker William Banting, who cut out sugars and starches in what was a precursor of the Atkins diet. An anonymous writer wrote, in 1883, that the average weight for a man of 5ft tall should be 8st 3lb, one of 5ft 6in tall 10st 7lb and one of 6ft 13st.

Another source of information about weight in the past is insurance records. Late nineteenth-century insurance companies were looking out for ways to judge the likely longevity of their applicants, and as part of this they weighed potential clients. There was an unspoken belief behind all this, of course, that overweight people were at a higher risk of mortality.

It should probably come as no surprise that the weight (and width!) of ordinary women in the past was of more interest than their height. The ideal Victorian woman was fleshy and full figured with wide hips and large

Lydia Cook, a Lancashire miner's wife, 1880s. Frequent childbearing took its toll on the shape of our female ancestors. She gave birth fourteen times; only four children survived. (Author's collection)

buttocks. But whatever her other dimensions, she was still supposed to be narrow around the middle. This was to be achieved not chiefly by diet or exercise but by wearing a corset. For decades a debate raged, with many magazine editors decrying the passion for narrower and narrower waists created by tight lace-up corsets. In November 1886 the editor of *The Girl's Own Paper* made this scathing reply to a woman calling herself 'Josephine', who had written in to complain about certain health problems:

Your symptoms point to tight lacing – red nose, spots, bad digestion etc. A fine woman with a handsome figure (say five feet five inches in height) should measure 26 inches round the waist, and in later life 28. Of course, a very small or very thin girl would naturally measure less. You know which description applies to yourself. The modern girl with a waist like a tobacco-pipe, and bulging out above and below like a bloated-looking spider, may solace herself with the assurance that her liver is cut in half, and that she would make an admirable specimen for a lecturer to decant upon. We advise her to bequeath her remains to some hospital for the benefit of science and the warning of others.

There were some anxieties about excess weight for women. By the mid-century clothes were being mass produced. Instead of the old made-to-measure garments, some clothes now came in standardised sizes – something that inevitably drew attention to expanding girths. By 1899 the popular *Sunlight Year Book* was declaring that a lady of 5ft 4in should weigh no more than 9st 4lb, a lady of 5ft 6in no more than 10st 4lb, and a lady of 6ft no more than 12st 12lb.

QUEEN VICTORIA – THE SHORT AND STOUT MONARCH

Queen Victoria was very short. At her accession in 1837 she was either 4ft 11in or 5ft (according to some more generous accounts). Apparently, when she went to visit Prime Minister Disraeli at his home in 1877, the queen asked for the legs of her chair to be cut short so that her feet would reach the floor. Though Victoria worried that her short stature might go against her with the British public, it seems unlikely that it had any effect on her popularity. By the end of her reign in 1901, the old queen had shrunk to a mere 4ft 7in.

As well as being short, Victoria was also rather overweight. From girlhood she loved her food, and was repeatedly warned by her advisers to lose weight. Her half-sister Feodora asked her not to eat so much at lunch or dinner and to take more exercise – but to no avail. In her forties the queen was tucking into four meals a day. She also ate very quickly. Since the plates of guests were taken away the moment the queen stopped eating, many visitors didn't get time to finish their meals when in her presence and went hungry.

When not attending royal banquets Victoria apparently liked nursery food. She began the day at 9.30 a.m. with porridge. Lunchtime, at 2 p.m., often included Brown Windsor soup made with shellfish, game and a dash of madeira wine. Afternoon tea was taken at 5.30 p.m. and then the evening meal at 8.30 p.m. At these times she would often consume haggis, red meat or chicken, and boiled potatoes. But she also had a terribly sweet tooth, with particular favourites being cranberry tart, chocolate cake, trifle, sponge cakes and ice creams. Though she disliked champagne, she enjoyed mulled wine and sweet ale, and increasingly partook of whisky, even adding it to her cups of tea.

While enjoying robust good health, the queen piled on weight, and by the 1880s she weighed 12st. Clothes were let out and stays were abandoned. At 19 the queen had had a 20in waist; by the end of her reign it has been estimated – from the size of her underwear – that she was a modern size 40!

THE TWENTIETH CENTURY

Excess weight continued to be a problem for the middle-class male at the turn of the twentieth century. In 1897 Queen Victoria's eldest son Bertie, later Edward VII, evidently taking after his mother, weighed 17st 12lb and had a 48in waist, statistics that ill-matched his 5ft 7in frame. By the 1930s diet surveys were documenting that middle-class professionals were eating too many calories a day (3,500–3,600 as opposed to the 2,700 recommended for sedentary workers). Many popular weight loss manuals were published and some diet foods were advertised. People were advised to eat and drink in moderation, to exercise regularly and to keep clean. They were also asked to chew their food properly and to maintain regular bowel movements. Health was starting to be seen as a patriotic necessity.

More mirrors in public places encouraged people to become critical of their personal appearance. People were weighed in doctors' surgeries and hospitals from the late nineteenth century. Large penny-operated electronic scales were invented in the 1880s, and were widely available in public places such as railway stations and restaurants in the 1920s and 1930s. Electronic bathroom scales were developed in the late 1940s, but it would not be until well after the Second World War that these were a common sight in British bathrooms.

In the early twentieth century, women were expected to be slimmer, and more emphasis was placed on exercise and an athletic physique. By the 1920s wealthier women were binding their breasts to achieve the slim flapper image; many were criticised for their haggard expressions and scrawny bodies. In the 1930s American divorcee Wallis Simpson, who stole the heart of the future King Edward VIII, made the notorious remark that a woman could 'never be too rich or too thin', revealing a disturbing propensity among middle- and upper-class women for slimming too much.

Everything changed with the advent of the Second World War. From this point until the early 1950s British families struggled to make rations last, no diet manuals were produced and no diet foods were manufactured. The regime of the war years and the years that followed reduced the population's intake of sugars, meats and fats and replaced them with bread, potatoes and meat. People were more active. Walking everywhere was common, since few had cars and petrol was rationed. During the war years the differentials that had previously existed between the weights of people in different classes disappeared.

Your ancestor's stature may or may not be worthy of note. But bear in mind that today women who are slim but not skinny are perceived as happier and more successful than their plumper (or more skeletal) counterparts. Research also claims that tall men are perceived as being more intelligent, socially skilled and successful than their shorter fellows, and have more chance of finding a mate and better employment prospects. So it is just possible that your ancestor's stature had some bearing on the way in which his or her life developed.

FIND OUT MORE

Roderick Floud, Kenneth Wachter and Annabel Gregory, *Height, Health and History: Nutritional Status in the United Kingdom, 1750–1980*, CUP, 1990.

Dr Louise Foxcroft, *Corsets and Calories: A History of Dieting Over 2000 Years*, Profile Books, 2012.

Anthony S. Wohl, *Endangered Lives: Public Health in Victorian Britain*, Harvard University Press, 1983.

brassgoggles.co.uk/forum/index.php?topic=2219.0 – discussion site about the height of the Victorians.

www.galtoninstitute.org.uk/Newsletters/GINL9912/francis_galton.htm – graphs showing distribution of height of Victorian Englishmen.

www.heightsite.com/4_tallest/4_tall-history.htm – fun facts about height around the world and in history.

8

Pinning them Down

BROOCHES

*G*littering diamonds, polished jet or dusty cameos – whatever their size, material or design, the old brooches lurking in your jewellery box may shed quite a bit of light on your family history. Brooches are perhaps more interesting than some other items of jewellery because they have traditionally been intimately connected with the business of family life, bought to mark major domestic events including births, engagements, weddings and even deaths. If the brooches themselves are no longer around, you may espy them in formal photographs taken in studios or at family occasions.

Brooches were often worn against the grain of fashion, out of sentiment or remembrance, or for some other reason known only to the wearer or those close to her. (*The Girl's Own Paper*, 1886)

BROOCHES IN PHOTOGRAPHS

If your ancestor is wearing more than one brooch in a photograph, she probably hoped that they would be noticed. One made for elegance; too many suggests vanity or eccentricity. Victorian novelist Mrs Gaskell (1810–65) delighted in describing the large number of brooches worn by the women of the Cheshire village of Cranford (in her novel of the same title, published in 1851). In this description brooches are seen as overindulgent and somewhat out of tune with fashion, but the reader feels that Mrs Gaskell loves her characters for them anyway:

> And with three new caps, and a greater array of brooches than had ever been seen together at one time since Cranford was a town, did Mrs Forrester, and Miss Matty, and Miss Pole appear on that memorable Tuesday evening. I counted seven brooches myself on Miss Pole's dress. Two were fixed negligently in her cap (one was a butterfly made of Scotch pebbles, which a vivid imagination might believe to be the real insect); one fastened her net neckerchief; one her collar; one ornamented the front of her gown, midway between her throat and waist; and another adorned the point of her stomacher. Where the seventh was I have forgotten, but it was somewhere about her, I am sure.

Brooches might be made of the latest materials and to fashionable designs, but they were more often seen as 'permanent ornaments', items that the owner would pin to her collar, lapel or shawl repeatedly throughout her life, to mark certain special occasions, rather than simply when the whim took her.

From the Royal Family downwards, the same brooch might be used, by one generation after another, to make a statement to the outside world. Queen Victoria's dazzling 'Fringe Brooch' was made for her by R. & S. Garrard & Co. in 1856 and was probably originally part of a fringe pattern *chaine-de-corsage*. It includes two impressive jewels presented to the queen by the Sultan of Turkey. The large emerald-cut central diamond is immediately surrounded by twelve brilliant cut diamonds, which are detachable from nine graduated pave-set chains of different lengths. Queen Victoria left the brooch to her son Edward VII, and it has subsequently been worn by Queen Alexandra, Queen Mary and Queen Elizabeth the Queen Mother. It was last worn by Queen Elizabeth II at a state banquet to honour the President of Turkey in November 2011 – an example of how the wearing of brooches can transcend fashion and rather reflect the significance of the occasion on which they are worn.

Often a few historical details can lead to far greater understanding of an ancestor in a photograph and her brooch. Newly married miner's wife Esther Wilkinson posed for a photograph shortly before the First World War, wearing a silver brooch at her throat shaped like a tennis racket, with the ball represented by a small diamond. The advent of electric lighting in some public buildings such as the Savoy Theatre in London in 1881 created a real passion for jewellery that sparkled at night. Esther Wilkinson would never have visited such grandiose places – her diamond is probably not

Esther Wilkinson wearing a tennis brooch with pride. In the late Victorian and early Edwardian periods, brooches were typically worn at the neck. (Author's collection)

even genuine – but her brooch is typical of its time, when smaller, lighter, more dazzling pieces were making their appearance as adornments to the shoulder. Esther's husband, Joseph Wilkinson, was a miner who spent time in the first decade of the twentieth century working in America; perhaps he brought the brooch home for her as an engagement or wedding present. It is still around, twinkling in the family jewellery box.

BROOCHES AND PAPERWORK

Brooches themselves are a tangible reminder of the past, but they have a greater importance for family history when there is paperwork connected with them; a letter or a will, for example, in which a particular piece of jewellery is described and perhaps even valued. There are frequent fascinating mentions of brooches in documents held in archives across Britain. These include reward notices for the finding of lost brooches, and descriptions of photographs in which brooches are important. Brooches were considered significant enough items of family property to be mentioned individually after a theft of jewellery. On 17 October 1820, for instance, John Hooper of Bodmin was sentenced to four months' hard labour in a house of correction for stealing a gold ring and a brooch, each valued at 6d.

Brooches have always had a special importance among inherited heirlooms, signifying degrees of affection between family members and friends. Indicative of status and wealth, they were left as legacies in wills or passed down less formally from mother to daughter or maiden aunt to niece. Many wills – particularly those relating to the aristocracy – make reference to brooches, and some of them were surprisingly valuable. The will of Lady Mary Charlotte Cooper of Middlesex made on 3 October 1831, for example, mentions a very large diamond brooch that had been given to Lady Cooper's father by the Nabob of Arcot. This brooch is the only personal possession listed, and it is mentioned alongside a property (26 Lower Brook Street, Grosvenor Square) – as if the two were possibly equivalent in value. (The will is to be found in Cheshire County Archives.) According to the testament, the brooch and the building were to be given to Lady Cooper's nephew, Sir George Baker, when he attained 21 years of age.

In her will of 8 May 1845 (now at Shropshire Archives) a rather more ordinary woman, Mary Ann Butler of Kensington Place, Clifton, Shropshire, left a fair number of brooches to her friends and family as follows: 'To Anne Iles Wilks her garnets and the garnet brooch with her (the testator's) mother's hair in it. To Harriett Cooper Butler, a pearl brooch with her (the testator's) late husband's hair in it. To Sarah, wife of William Baylis of Stroud, her pearl brooch of an oval shape. To Careline [sic] Besley a pearl brooch in the shape of a crescent.' These brooches are listed in order of value: the closer the relationship between Mary Ann Butler and her beneficiary, the more valuable the brooch that she bequeathed. No doubt many brooches like these became the subject of family jealousies and petty disputes.

REAL BROOCHES

There have been brooches (or fibulas as they were earlier known) in Britain since the age of the Vikings; indeed, during the ninth and tenth centuries bronze, oval brooches were mass-produced in clay moulds, and were often elaborately designed with amber and glass beads. These brooches – like those that followed them down through the centuries – nearly always served a double purpose; they were decorative and also served as a means of fastening women's dresses.

The interesting brooches you are likely to find in your family jewellery box were probably made in the Victorian era or early twentieth century. Traditionally brooches from the nineteenth century were made from metal of one sort or another and decorated with enamel or gemstones. As Mrs Gaskell humorously recorded of the brooches of her Cranford women, there were a huge variety of shapes and forms, 'some with dogs' eyes painted in them; some that were like small picture-frames with mausoleums and weeping-willows neatly executed in hair inside; some, again, with miniatures of ladies and gentlemen sweetly smiling out of a nest of stiff muslin'.

Fashions in brooches – just as in so many other aspects of dress – changed frequently, and this allows experts quite easily to date their manufacture to a particular period. Once you have selected an interesting brooch from your collection, you should consider the size, the design, the clasp and the material from which it is made. To correctly date it, you should consult an expert or one of the books mentioned in the Find Out More section at the end of this chapter, but the following tips may give you a start in understanding when, and perhaps even why, a particular piece came into your family's possession.

Jewellery with Scottish motifs became very popular after 1848, when Queen Victoria purchased Balmoral Castle. At this time circular Scottish plaid pins (or target brooches) were fashionable, as were brooches with heraldic crests, dirks and claymores (knives and swords), thistles and St Andrew's crosses. Such items tended to be made out of agates, malachites, cairngorms (dark tallow-amber faceted quartz) and amethysts.

Brooches became much bigger from the 1850s onwards. This is because the fashion of the day was for voluminous skirts supported by crinolines, and such enormous dresses required larger jewellery. Working-class women wore brooches that had been mass-produced by machines. Electroplated trinkets set with glass stones were often made to resemble gold and diamonds. Popular working-class brooches were made from silver coins, upon which the name of a family member might have been engraved. Others, known as 'message brooches', had motifs with particular meanings:

Forget-me-not – *remembrance*
Ivy – *friendship*
Anchor – *hope*
Cross – *faith*
Heart – *charity*
Horseshoe- *good luck*
Love birds – *love*

After Queen Victoria became Empress of India in 1876 there was a fashion for jewels from exotic places, including Mughal jewellery, Jaipur enamel and gold-mounted tigers' claws from Calcutta. By the 1880s heavy, sombre jewellery was losing favour, and lighter, more delicate pieces took its place. Brooches became smaller and were often worn in multiples, with silver replacing gold for daytime wear. Many brooches became more utilitarian in design, as they were needed as fasteners for veils, hats and bodices. At this time brooches became known as 'handy pins' or 'beauty pins'.

Jubilee brooches celebrating Queen Victoria's sixty years on the throne and marked 'VR', together with the dates 1837 and 1897 were popular at the end of the century. Other brooches signalled (by lettering or insignia) that their owners were members of particular clubs or societies.

Brooches became more intricate and elegant in design from the start of the twentieth century. Fashions for how to wear brooches changed as well: pins were worn at the waist and later at the shoulder. Platinum, a strong and ductile material, was frequently used, rather than silver or gold. Many brooches had a filigree or lacy effect, and stones were set on open-backed mounts to allow light to shine through the jewel from all sides.

Edwardian brooches tended to be monochromatic, in whites or pastel colours. Diamonds were frequently used, as were pearls and moonstones. Other popular stones in early twentieth-century jewellery were peridots, garnets, tourmalines, amethysts, synthetic rubies (from 1902) and synthetic sapphires (from 1911). The first patented safety catch on brooches appeared in the Arts and Crafts jewellery of the Edwardian period. Such jewellery brought together cheaper materials and a high degree of craftsmanship.

More brooches were made out of white gold during the First World War, when platinum was appropriated for military usages. Handmade novelty brooches made from ceramic, felt, yarn and feathers may date from the Second World War, when many factories were given over to the war effort. Some of these represented popular movie stars; others were carvings of exotic Oriental or African faces.

SPECIAL BROOCHES

There have, of course, been an enormous number of different kinds of brooch made over the last 200 years or so, but three popular types that potentially tell a special tale deserve mention here.

MOURNING BROOCHES

In the Victorian era – and particularly after the death of Queen Victoria's beloved husband Albert in 1861 – it was usual for a period of mourning to be entered after a loved one died. Wearing black became fashionable. During this time people wore dark jewellery – including brooches. Those made from Whitby jet were suitable for the first period of so-called 'deep mourning'. Other mourning brooches had compartments in which the hair of the deceased person could be displayed. Brooches made of Bakelite (in imitation of jet) were also worn by those lower down the social scale. By the 1920s the idea of wearing such mourning jewellery was considered ghoulish and outdated.

SUFFRAGETTE BROOCHES

Made in the early years of the twentieth century, these should be differentiated from suffragette badges. Women who wished to proclaim their affiliation to the suffrage movement wore badges, while those who needed to keep their allegiances more discreet wore brooches. These were recognisable as suffragette items only by their colours: green (for hope), white (for purity) and violet (for dignity). The initials of these colours stood for **G**ive **W**omen the **V**ote, and they were the colours of the key political organisation – the Women's Social and Political Union. Suffragette brooches characteristically included tourmalines, amethysts, peridots, seed pearls, moonstones and enamel, and were made in a variety of designs.

While colour was more important than design in suffragette brooches, some of the designs were also representative of the movement's aims. Some brooches, for example, incorporated a bar and chain, since chains were a symbol of oppression. At other times ribbons in green, white and violet were added to ordinary brooches to indicate sympathy with the movement.

One special kind of suffragette brooch – the Holloway brooch – was designed by Emmeline Pankhurst. This was given to suffragettes who had been jailed in London's Holloway prison. It had an enamelled green, white and purple arrow mounted on a silver reproduction of the portcullis at the jail. If you have one of these in your family jewellery box you may find that it is worth quite a lot of money.

SWEETHEART BROOCHES

Sweetheart brooches were given by servicemen in both the First and Second World Wars to their loved ones. These were often in the form of a miniature version of the regimental badge and they often had gems inset. Some had an ensign, aircraft or wings.

Bear in mind that a brooch can provide an excellent prompt or talking point when you are interviewing elderly relatives about your family history. Ask your great-aunt about the particularly attractive brooch that fastens her cardigan, and you may well be treated to a quite unexpected revelation or family story.

FIND OUT MORE

Joan Evans, *A History of Jewellery, 1100–1870*, Dover Publications, 1990.

Charlotte Gere, *Victorian Jewellery Design*, William Kimber, 1972.

Graham Hughes, *Pictorial History of Gems and Jewellery*, Phaidon Press, 1978.

Helen Muller, *Jet Jewellery and Ornaments*, Shire Publications, 1994.

Helen Reynolds, *A Fashionable History Of Jewellery and Accessories*, Heinemann Library, 2004.

www.khulsey.com/jewelry/jewelry_history_victorian.html – on jewellery of the Georgian, Victorian and Edwardian periods.

www.whitbyjet.co.uk/history.html – the Whitby Jet Heritage Centre history page.

www.youtube.com/watch?v=GxSONDKa3Ik and www.youtube.com/watch?v=f4Hcvrqa4kA – short videos on how to distinguish between Victorian and Edwardian brooches by comparing the clasps.

9

All Fastened Up

BUTTONS

*I*t is not so long ago that every home kept a button box. More valued – and less easily replaced in the past than they are today – buttons were often kept even when the original garments to which they belonged had long since been discarded. If you have a button box sort through it carefully; it may be the starting point for more than one line of enquiry into your family history.

Among the modern, faceless plastic buttons and wooden toggles, be prepared to discover some little gems. Buttons that you might have inherited from the mid-Victorian period will delight you with their variety of textures, colours and designs – and, indeed, this is one reason why so many of them were kept. Over the centuries buttons have been made in an amazing variety of materials and designs. The most common kind are the 'flat' or 'sew-through' buttons in which holes in the button itself allow it to be attached to the cloth. 'Shank' buttons have a bar at the back through which the thread is sewn. 'Covered' buttons are encased in fabric that is secured in place by a separate back piece.

Buttons have been made from all sorts of materials, including shell, bone, ivory, cloth, glass, stone, horn, leather, ceramic, celluloid and wood, as well as every type of metal from iron to gold. And in their designs buttons have reflected the interests and fads of their times, with engravings, paintings and enamelled depictions of all manner of things from animals to architecture. Some buttons, known as 'realistics', have even been shaped like the items they portray – anything and everything from flowers and fruit to faces and planes.

The family button tin may be the starting point for some fascinating stories. (Author's collection)

You might also come across a monogrammed button from the uniform of an ancestor who was a soldier, a policeman, a worker in a bank or a tram driver. And there may be grimmer secrets too. The inmates of orphanages, workhouses and asylums often had uniforms with their own distinctive buttons. Many buttons are relatively easy to identify, and can set you on the path to discovering more about your ancestors' lives through military, institutional and company records.

A BRIEF HISTORY OF BUTTONS

Buttons have been around for hundreds of years, replacing the ties and pins of ancient history. Many ancient burials included buttons or button-like objects, and it seems that as early as the Bronze Age large buttons were being used to fasten cloaks. Nevertheless, laces and hooks were the main methods of fastening garments until the end of the sixteenth century.

Buttons, however, continued as decoration, and from the sixteenth to the nineteenth centuries increased in size and became ever more elaborate, sometimes incorporating precious metals and jewels.

The oldest buttons in the average family button box may possibly date back as far as the mid-nineteenth century. It was not until Victoria's reign that vast improvements in manufacturing techniques meant that buttons could be mass-produced, first by hand and later by machine, in an extraordinary range of synthetic materials and designs. Having been very much the provenance of men in the eighteenth century, the button became a part of ladies' fashion in the Victorian period. Before 1840 women's dresses tended to be hooked or laced, although handmade thread or Dorset buttons (stitched over moulds or wire) were used on linen and ladies' underwear. By the 1850s buttons were very much part of outer wear, and were used both for functional and for decorative purposes.

Buttons proved a useful way of making a living for many of our ancestors, and the greatest site of the British button-making industry was in the Midlands. Most employees were women and children, since the manufacture of buttons required a large number of simple but repetitive processes that did not necessitate the skills of trained craftsmen. As Harriet Martineau (sometimes referred to as the first female sociologist) put it in an article entitled 'What There is in a Button', in *Household Words*, April 1852, 'It is wonderful, is it not? That on that small pivot turns the fortunes of such multitudes of men, women and children, in so many parts of the world; that such industry, and so many fine faculties, should be brought out and exercised by so small a thing as a button.'

Early gilt buttons were covered with a thin layer of gold leaf or silver, and later dipped in one of these two metals. But at the beginning of the Victorian period metal buttons fell out of fashion and were replaced by buttons made of new materials, such as jet, ivory, glass, bone, horn, and even nuts specially imported from South America. Some of these were then covered by silk or linen. Fancier buttons were made from shell and tortoiseshell and boasted jewels and cameos. There were also tintype buttons into which pictures were inserted and buttons made from crocheted thread and covered with embroidered fabric. By the 1850s buttons were being made, at least in part, by machine. A particular pretty and fashionable design of the 1850s was the acorn button, which required a number of different processes to achieve completion as Harriet Martineau described:

Here is one shaping in copper the nut of the acorn: another is shaping the cup. Disks of various degrees of concavity, sugar-loaves, and many other shapes, are dropping by thousands from the machines into the troughs below. And here is the covering or pressing machine again at work – here covering the nut of the acorn with green satin, and there casing the cup with green Florentine; and finally fitting and fastening them together, so that no ripening and loosening touch of time shall, as in the case of the natural acorn, cause them to drop apart.

From the 1880s through to the end of the Edwardian era women's and children's clothing often sported picture buttons. Some common themes were art and literature, children's stories, natural history, music, architecture and mythology. For men's clothing there were uniform buttons, buttons with coats of arms, livery buttons, club buttons and service buttons. Pearl buttons, used to fasten the most expensive fashions, were a special case, and were manufactured in small workshops where the material was worked by hand rather than by machine. Mother of pearl, abalone and mollusc shells – including yellow-lip oyster shells from the West Coast of Australia – were used to make these buttons.

Respectable Victorian ancestors wore plenty of buttons. Wealthy ladies dazzled in dresses with long rows of twenty buttons or more, and there were buttons on boots and gloves too. Getting dressed could be a lengthy process, requiring the help of others or the assistance of a button hook. Heavily buttoned garments helped to confirm Victorian ideals of prudishness and restraint, though buttons could also symbolise secrecy and hidden sexuality. Buttoned corsets and other garments were fetishised in the underworld of Victorian pornographic literature.

By contrast with wealthy women, the Victorian poor could afford few buttons. In 1849 the journalist Henry Mayhew (1812–87) was asked by the *Morning Chronicle* to be its Metropolitan correspondent for a series entitled *Labour and the Poor*. He interviewed a 38-year-old former cotton spinner and soldier who was now a street vagrant. Notice how this fellow's paucity of buttons is crucial to the description of his poverty: 'He was tall, and had been florid-looking (judging from his present complexion). His coat – very old and worn, and once black – would not button, and would have hardly held together if buttoned. He was out at elbows, and some parts of the collar were pinned together. His waistcoat was of a match with his coat, and his trousers were rags. He had some shirt, as was evident by his waistcoat,

This folding button hook made from polished steel was used by millworker Emma McGowan, probably at the turn of the twentieth century. On one side is the word 'Mandoline', describing the mandolin shape of the hook when opened, and on the other 'Depose' (close). (With thanks to Mrs Pat Doney)

held together by one button. A very dirty handkerchief was tied carelessly round his neck.'

After the death of Prince Albert in 1861 Queen Victoria started to wear black jet buttons in mourning for him. A fashion was born. Those people who couldn't afford jet had buttons made from black glass. Find out how wealthy your ancestors were by placing an inherited black button in a glass of water. If it floats it is probably jet; if it sinks it is glass.

With the advent of machines, the numbers of our ancestors involved in the button trade declined considerably. In Birmingham the number of employees dropped from 17,000 in 1830 to about 6,000 forty years later.

In the Edwardian period the portly shape of King Edward VII led to a fashion among men for leaving the bottom button of a suit jacket undone. The new fashion for single-breasted dinner jackets among the upper classes required only one button, which was also usually left undone, thus requiring a cummerbund to cover the waistband of trousers. Buttons in the early twentieth century became much simpler in design, reflecting the large number of white-collar workers. By the 1930s most buttons were made from plastic, and while some delightful buttons from this era undoubtedly exist, the heyday of the button was over.

IDENTIFYING BUTTONS

If you have an interesting button that you feel may yield more information about your family history, you should have a go at dating it. The British Button Society has produced a very interesting downloadable booklet which includes many ideas about how to test for the material of your button: www.nationalbuttonsociety.org/Beginners_Booklet.html.

Pewter ones, for example, will leave a pencil-like mark when drawn across a piece of paper, a drop of water placed on a jade button will draw in rather than spread out, and plastic buttons give a duller sound when clicked on the teeth than other materials such as glass, china and stone. Some button connoisseurs will test for materials using an electric hot needle inserted into the back of the button: the material can be deduced from the resulting smell – horn, like cooking meat or burning feathers; jet, like coal; tortoiseshell, like stagnant salt water.

Once you have a few ideas about the material of your button you might contact the British Button Society at www.britishbuttonsociety.org., where you can send images of your button identification. Alternatively, you might find that someone else on the site has a similar button. It is also worth taking a look at other websites. Think laterally here; some of the best websites on the subject are not obviously to do with buttons or family history but to do with metal detecting! Try, for instance, www.colchestertreasurehunting.co.uk, which displays photographs and descriptions of thousands of buttons. As well as online references, there are also many books on buttons. Compare your finds with their pictures. A short list appears in the Find Out More section at the end of this chapter, but there are plenty of others.

BUTTONS THAT TELL THEIR OWN TALE

Some buttons tell a story of their own. Those with strong identifying marks such as the name of a company or an easily recognisable design will often have been worn by the men in your family. These are the buttons that were worn on uniforms of one sort or another. They may lead you to discover that your ancestor was in service, in the military or in some sort of government occupation.

LIVERY BUTTONS

These buttons were worn on the uniforms of servants in large English households. They often featured eagles and other birds of prey. Sometimes these had associations with a family name – a cockerel for 'Cockburn', for example, or a hawk for 'Hawksley'. Those working in the service of dukes, earls, barons and viscounts may have worn livery buttons with a coronet pictured on them. Other buttons bore crests and shields, the motto of the employing family, animals such as elephants chosen to denote strength and courage, mythological creatures, or inanimate objects such as scales. To check out the details of a family crest from England, Ireland, Scotland or Wales see www.familycrestuk.co.uk.

MILITARY AND NAVY BUTTONS

These buttons range from small examples, which may have been used to secure the chinstraps on helmets, to large ones, worn on greatcoats, tunics and service dress jackets. British regiments were numbered from 1751 to 1881, and a button with a number can be very useful in helping you identify to which regiment an ancestor belonged. The more recent 'general service' buttons that were worn from 1881 until after the First World War are less helpful, however, since the same plain design was used across the military. Far more interesting are officers' buttons, which were made to a higher specification, have regimental patterns and are often mounted.

In the First World War brass buttons, sometimes plated with gold, were considered vital to the morale of a regiment, and when required could be sent to the Allied Front

Private Wilfred Wilkinson (1896–1917) of the Royal Marine Brigade and later the 1st Royal Marine Battalion, Royal Marine Light Infantry. Soldiers in the First World War sewed on and cleaned their own buttons. Being properly buttoned up was a matter of regimental pride. (Author's collection)

within eight hours of notice being given. Improperly buttoned soldiers could be reprimanded, and those soldiers subjected to court martial for other reasons could be 'de-buttoned'.

OTHER SERVICE BUTTONS

Different police constabularies across Britain have traditionally had their insignia stamped on buttons, and many had in their centre the crown of the monarch at any given time. Firemen from the 1880s to the 1930s wore buttons that were standardised across the country. These bore a helmet and two axes. There were twelve large buttons arranged in two rows down the front of the tunic, two smaller ones on the epaulettes, two more on the back of the tunic and two on the breast pockets. Fire services had different cap badges and buttons from 1947 onwards. Many companies in the early twentieth century had their own internal fire teams. The Co-op, for example, had its own brigade set up mainly to ensure fire prevention rather than to fight fires, and Co-op firemen had uniforms that sported distinctive buttons.

COMPANY AND INSTITUTIONAL BUTTONS

There may be a button in your box that will alert you to the fact that your ancestor worked for a bank or other financial institution, a motor or transport company, a hospital or asylum, a hotel, a utility or public company, a waterway, the Post Office, or many other types of company. Some of these bear embossed designs: employees of Lloyds Bank, for example, wore buttons that carried a border of beehives arranged around a winged horse, while employees of the Irish Post Office sported buttons with wreathed harps. Other buttons bear acronyms: 'RR' may be readily identifiable as Rolls Royce Limited, but you may need some help in attributing 'GSC' to the Glasgow Salvage Corps! For plenty more examples see www.goldenagebuttons.co.uk/lists/Companies.htm.

OTHER BUTTONS

Many buttons bear no lettering or insignia and therefore tell no obvious tale. They may still, however, give you the flavour of the way a life was lived. You might come across one that obviously belonged to a special dress or outfit, a mother-of-pearl button, for example, from a great-aunt's ballgown. Just from the size, material and design of buttons like these, you might learn something about your ancestor's status and aspirations.

Don't underestimate the power of buttons to stimulate interest in your family's history. There is certainly no better way of getting young children interested than to let them rummage through the family button box and tell them the stories that arise, and as prompts to the memories of older family members such buttons can be invaluable. Fragments of information, such as 'this was from mother's wedding gown' or 'mother wore a coat with these buttons when she first arrived in Britain' can lead you to otherwise hidden stories from your family's past.

FIND OUT MORE

Dennis Blair, *British Buttons: Civilian Uniform Buttons 19th–20th Century*, Greenlight Publishing, 2001.

Michael J. Cuddeford, Alan Meredith, Gillian Meredith, *Identifying Buttons*, Mount Publications, 1997.

Nina Edwards, *On The Button, the Significance of An Ordinary Item*, I.B. Tauris, 2011.

Primrose Peacock, *Discovering Old Buttons*, Shire Publications, 2008.

Howard Ripley, *Police Buttons*, Police Insignia Collectors Association of Great Britain, 2000.

Robert Wilkinson-Latham, *Discovering British Military Badges and Buttons*, Shire, 2005.

www.britishbuttonsociety.org – British Button Society.

www.mandacrafts.co.uk/Dorset%20Button%20History.pdf – the history of the Dorset button.

www.nationalbuttonsociety.org/NBS_Publications_&_Forms_files/ NBS%20Beginners%20Booklet.doc – downloadable Beginners' Booklet of the National Button Society, which gives advice on how to sort, identify and even display your buttons.

www.homepage.ntlworld.com/mike.comerford/ORDNANCE/29.htm – useful site for identifying military buttons from their designs, finishes, fasteners and size.

10

Just the Thing

RINGS

*I*f you have inherited a wedding or engagement ring, you have also inherited a crucial part of your family's history. A ring is at once the property of an individual and a symbol of a union; a reminder of two ancestors rather than one. Circular-shaped to represent eternity and with a hole in the middle to symbolise the unknown future, rings may be a validation or an irony, depending on which way your ancestors' romantic relationship progressed.

Many Victorian women – particularly the less well off – wore a wedding ring only, and since divorce was very difficult to obtain for most of the

This platinum and diamond ring started out as a gentleman's dress ring in the early twentieth century. It became a lady's engagement ring in 1961. (Author's collection)

population until the 1960s, it is probable that such an item graced your ancestor's hand from the day of her marriage right through to the day of her death. Bar removing it for a bit of baking or bathing, it is unlikely that she took it off even in widowhood: removing nuptial rings at any point was thought to be unlucky. If the swollen fingers of old age did not force her to remove it, then it may be that it parted from her only at her death – a time when rings were customarily prised from the fingers by grieving or (occasionally) greedy relatives. Engagement rings may have had a less straightforward past than wedding rings. The breakdown of a betrothal was signalled by the return of a ring, or a ring may have been retained by a spurned fiancée despite the dissolution of a relationship.

PHOTOGRAPHS: IS SHE (OR HE) WEARING A RING?

A common question when trying to date a family photograph is whether or not one of the sitters is wearing an engagement or wedding ring. Indeed, sometimes we judge the quality of a photograph on whether or not a wedding or engagement ring can be properly distinguished. Late nineteenth-century wedding and engagement photographs often give prominence to the woman's left hand (sometimes it rests against the back of a chair or on top of a book), with the new ring displayed prominently. You may need to use a microscope to check this properly.

But trying to date a photograph with reference to the wearing of rings is likely to be an unsatisfactory exercise. Engagement rings were not commonly worn until the end of the nineteenth century and only graced the fingers of the majority of our female ancestors from the 1940s onwards. Moreover, deeply religious people across a variety of denominations have at certain times believed that the wearing of a wedding ring (even a plain gold band) was contrary to the principles of modesty and simplicity that should govern the lives of good Christians. In the nineteenth century ancestors who were Quakers, for example, would not have worn a wedding ring.

If a male ancestor appears not to be wearing a wedding ring in a family photograph, do not presume that he isn't married. Although brides have worn wedding rings since medieval times, few grooms wore rings as a sign of marital status before the mid-twentieth century. Jewellery in the Victorian period was almost exclusively the property of women. Widowers sometimes kept hold of their wives' wedding rings until their own death.

The Victorian poet Robert Browning (1812–89), for example, wore the wedding ring of his wife, the poet Elizabeth Barrett Browning, on his watch chain from the day she died in 1861 until his own death twenty-eight years later. From 1939 many men going off to fight in the Second World War wore a ring to remind them of their wives and families back home. More rings have been worn by men since the 1960s, as jewellery for men in general has become more socially acceptable. On top of this, the advent of women's rights, particularly from the 1970s onwards, has encouraged more wives to insist that their husbands wear a wedding ring.

WOMEN AND THE SYMBOLISM OF WEDDING RINGS

The little band of gold on the third finger of our ancestor's left hand carried a cultural meaning far greater than its tiny size. In the nineteenth century and beyond, being married was a symbol of romantic and economic success for both sexes. For a woman, being married and having a family were seen as the surest way to social acceptance and happiness. In the early part of the century being married also signified that you had effectively become as one entity with your husband under the law – useful if you committed a murder, since you could not stand trial alone. Less useful if you owned any property in your own right, as once married you effectively handed it and all rights appertaining to it, as well as all rights to your children, to your husband, should you separate.

For some intellectual women the wedding ring was an uneasy symbol – a tribute to a romantic union on the one hand and a ball and chain representing economic and sexual disadvantage on the other. Charlotte Brontë's Jane Eyre, from the novel of the same name (1848), whose wedding to Mr Rochester was so dramatically halted just as the ring was to be put upon her finger, turns down the offer of a loveless marriage to her cousin St John Rivers, knowing that the placing of a ring on her finger would make her his sexual possession: 'Can I receive from him the bridal ring, endure all the forms of love (which I doubt not he would scrupulously observe) and know that the spirit was quite absent?'

Wedding rings were such powerful indicators of societal approval that they were occasionally worn by our ancestors even when a marriage had not been entered into. For unmarried mothers in the past, the wearing of a wedding ring could automatically convey respectability, creating the impression that they were widows rather than whores. Mrs Gaskell's heroine Ruth in the novel of the same name (1853) is given such a ring by Miss Benson for just this purpose:

> She pulled out an old wedding-ring, and hurried it on Ruth's finger. Ruth hung down her head, and reddened deep with shame; her eyes smarted with the hot tears that filled them. Miss Benson talked on, in a nervous hurried way –
>
> 'It was my grandmother's; it's very broad; they made them so then, to hold a posy inside: there's one in that – "Thine own sweetheart Till death doth part," I think it is. There, there! Run away, and look as if you'd always worn it.'
>
> Ruth went up to her room, and threw herself down on her knees by the bedside, and cried as if her heart would break.

A tiny minority of our married women ancestors refused to wear wedding rings for feminist reasons. Lancashire woman Elizabeth Wolstenholme (1833–1918), for example, was a Victorian advocate of women's education and was instrumental in getting the Married Women's Property Act of 1882 (a law allowing a married woman to retain her own property after marriage) and the Custody of Infants Act, 1886 (a law giving separated women more rights over their children) passed in Parliament. She became pregnant by the poet Benjamin Elmy in 1874, and because, it seems, of the disapprobation of some of her fellow campaigners for women's rights, married him in a civil ceremony in Kensington Register Office later in the year. But she declined to wear a wedding ring or take his name.

Symbolic value aside, for the poor, wedding rings were a valuable form of property that could usefully be pawned in times of hardship. For working-class women, pawning was a way of exerting power in the household economy and the wedding ring, since it was an item of personal decoration that benefited no one but the wife, was often the first thing to go. It is possible that your ancestor's wedding ring went back and forth to the local pawn shop as she struggled to make ends meet. It has been estimated that in 1866 alone, there were more than 29 million transactions in the pawnbrokers' shops of Metropolitan London: many of these will have been undertaken by women and will have involved items of personal jewellery. At times of deep economic depression, such as the early 1880s (and later in the 1930s), more women pawned their wedding rings than ever before. Real wedding rings were replaced with curtain rings or other temporary

The artist of this drawing has taken care to include a wedding ring on the finger of the mother of the baby – for the sake of propriety. (*Love-Light, being the extra Christmas number of the Girl's Own Paper*, 1891)

bands until the original item could be bought back. Sometimes economic circumstances meant that this was never possible.

Later in the nineteenth century the business of wearing a wedding ring could have other economic connotations for women: it could be an instant bar on paid work. Those affected tended to be educated, middle- and lower-middle-class women in teaching and clerical jobs rather than those in more menial occupations. The Post Office was one employer that operated the marriage bar – preventing women from working in so-called 'established' positions from 1876 to 1946 – although exceptions were made during both world wars. In such circumstances wearing a wedding ring could mean the difference between getting a job and not getting one. It is possible that some of our female ancestors removed their wedding rings just so that they could go to work.

One salutary story about wedding rings and women's work concerns the case of Judith Hubback – a twentieth-century campaigner for better employment rights for women. Judith gained a first-class honours degree in history from Newnham College, Cambridge in 1936 and later a diploma in education at London University. In 1939 she married the economist David Hubback, and soon after applied for a teaching job at the City of London School for Girls. All was going well in the interview until one of the interviewers noticed that she was wearing a wedding ring; she was immediately disqualified from the application process. The experience had a profound effect on Hubback. Appalled by the way in which many intellectual women like herself were unable to achieve their potential in a male-dominated society, she went on to become a highly acclaimed analytical psychologist, and wrote several books on the subject of women's exclusion from meaningful work.

INHERITED WEDDING AND ENGAGEMENT RINGS – WHAT TO LOOK FOR

If an engagement or wedding ring has ended up in your possession, it's worth trying to find out from family members how it got there. The 'back stories' of rings can make interesting telling. It has been common, for instance, for brides to wear engagement or wedding rings that belonged to their deceased mothers-in-law or other women in their husband's families. The current Duchess of Cambridge's blue sapphire engagement ring first belonged to her mother-in-law Princess Diana, for example. Other rings have been passed down to children bearing the same name as the original owner. One family history researcher notes that in her family a particular ring was passed on to each new 'Margaret' in the family; another recalls a ring that was passed on to girls in the family as each one reached her sixteenth birthday.

Simple wedding bands were usually made of gold, although there was at least one historical period (the seventeenth century) when Italian silver was favoured. Traditionally, if a couple could not afford a gold ring they might borrow one for the ceremony. Since wedding rings tended to be a perfect fit, if nothing else, your inherited ring will tell you one thing for certain about your ancestor – the size of his or her ring finger! Rings that were too tight were superstitiously believed to foretell the break-up of a relationship because of jealousy, while those that were too loose might signal a future parting of the ways.

Engagement rings might have more to tell us about our ancestor than wedding rings, indicating, for instance, something about her fashion-consciousness, class status or wealth. From the 1930s it was commonly assumed that the price of an engagement ring should equal the groom's gross monthly salary – no mean feat for most couples. Later this was doubled to twice his monthly salary. While few couples perhaps managed this, engagement rings have nevertheless always been one of the most valuable of family heirlooms. Such items of jewellery acted as a kind of surety to the bride that a wedding would actually take place. In Britain the gift of an engagement ring was, and still is, presumed to be an absolute gift to the fiancée. If the wedding is called off she is allowed to keep it, unless it can be proved that it was given on condition that it would be returned if the marriage did not take place.

Originally only the wealthiest nobles could afford elaborate designs or precious stones for their engagement rings, and most early ones were simple metal bands. It was only in the late nineteenth and early twentieth centuries that relatively ordinary ancestors could afford more decorative engagement rings, containing precious stones.

Your great-grandmother may have chosen an engagement ring with a stone that represented her birth month, or the month in which she became engaged or was to get married (a popular trend in Victorian times). These traditional British birthstones were defined by the National Association of Goldsmiths in 1937:

January – garnet	July – ruby
February – amethyst	August – peridot
March – aquamarine	September – sapphire
April – diamond	October – opal
May – emerald	November – topaz
June – pearl	December – turquoise

Alternatively a bride might have chosen a stone – budget allowing – that chimed in with the contemporary fashions in gem jewellery, often headed up by the women of the British Royal Family or famous beauties of the times.

DIAMONDS

These were used in rings from the thirteenth century and were traditionally worn only by royalty. After their discovery in South African mines in 1867, however, diamonds became much more easily available. As a result, they dropped in price and soon became a firm favourite of the middle classes. In 1886 Tiffany and Co. introduced the Solitaire Tiffany setting, in which a single diamond was held by six claws. The De Beers advertising campaign of 1947, which featured the slogan 'Diamonds are Forever', brought this stone more firmly to the attention of the masses. So popular did diamonds become that very rich families of the last two centuries often turned to other gemstones in rings to demonstrate their superior wealth.

EMERALDS

These stones, ranging in colour from yellow-green to blue-green, were believed to have great healing powers that could cure everything from leprosy to dysentery. Queen Victoria's engagement ring from Prince Albert (in 1839) was a snake with an emerald-set head – an item of jewellery that set off a trend for serpent-shaped engagement rings. Society beauty Jackie Bouvier received an emerald engagement ring from John F. Kennedy in 1953.

SAPPHIRES

These symbolised romantic love, truth and commitment. An ancient but commonly held myth was that the stone's colour would change or fade if it was worn by an untruthful person. Sapphires were also particularly popular in engagements that took place in the Edwardian period (1901–10). Royals who have favoured sapphires in their engagement rings include the Queen Mother (1923), Princess Diana (1981) and the Duchess of Cambridge (2010).

RUBIES

The king of gems and symbol of romance, the ruby has been a favourite stone in royal rings for at least a couple of centuries. Queen Victoria was given a ruby ring by her half-sister Feodora on the occasion of her wedding to Prince Albert in 1840. In more recent years rubies have graced the engagement rings of Princess Margaret (to Anthony Armstrong Jones, 1960), Princess Anne (to Mark Philips, 1973) and Sarah Ferguson, Duchess of York (to Prince Andrew, 1986).

MULTI-STONE RINGS

If your inherited ring includes several different gemstones, it may be an example of a Victorian 'poesy' ring. Some of these included the birthstones of the engaged couple and those of each of their parents. In others, the initial letters of the gemstones chosen spelt out the bride's name or a message (for example, **L**apis lazuli, **O**pal, **V**ermarine and **E**merald for **LOVE** or **D**iamond, **E**merald, **A**methyst and **R**uby for **DEAR**). Such rings may also have had messages or lines of poetry engraved on their outer or inner surfaces.

RINGS AND DEATH

If your family wedding ring has disappeared altogether, consider the fact that it might have been buried along with your ancestor. While it has been the tradition of Western Christian funerals not to bury 'grave goods' along with a corpse, wedding rings have sometimes been an exception to this. One of the most famous people to be buried with a wedding ring was Queen Victoria, who died in 1901. In addition to Prince Albert's dressing gown and cloak and sundry other items of jewellery, the queen requested that she be buried wearing a wedding ring belonging to the mother of her favourite ghillie, John Brown. The presence of the ring in the coffin has fuelled speculation that Victoria married Brown in secret.

Wedding and engagement rings have sometimes been used as a guide to identifying bodies after sudden death or tragedy far from home. A wedding ring, for instance, recently turned up among the wreckage of what appears to have been an RAF Lancaster bomber shot down on D-Day (1944) near Carentan in northern Normandy. Among other personal items, including a silver-plated cigarette case, a watch and three RAF woollen jumpers, aviation archaeologists found a mangled ring in a nearby marsh bearing the initials 'A.C.' and the engraved inscription 'Love Vera'. Further research confirmed that the ring belonged to a gunner and wireless operator named Albert Chambers, who married Vera Grubb at St Giles's Church, Normanton, near Derby, in 1943, just eight months before he was shot down at the untimely age of 23. In this case it was the ring, rather than any other artefact or evidence, that led to the identification of the wreck and its crew.

FIND OUT MORE

Rachel Church, *Rings*, V&A Publishing, 2012.

Joan Evans, *A History of Jewellery, 1100–1870*, Faber and Faber, 1953.

Diana Scarisbrick, *Rings – Jewellery of Love, Power and Devotion*, Thames and Hudson, 2007.

Diana Scarisbrick, *Rings – Symbols of Wealth*, Harry N. Abrams, 1993.

www.bigbeadlittlebead.com – guide to traditional and alternative British birthstones.

www.everything-wedding-rings.com/history-of-wedding-rings.html – for a helpful guide on dating nineteenth- and twentieth-century rings.

www.postalheritage.org.uk/page/women – on the way in which the marriage bar affected women working in the Post Office.

11

Links to the Past

CUFFLINKS

'Bachelor buttons', 'sleeve links' or *boutons de manchette* – cufflinks, (by whatever name they have been known), have long been a favoured celebratory gift for male relatives. And, like other items of inherited jewellery, the value of these small, decorative items to you now might be more than purely financial. The way in which your ancestor tied his cuffs might actually provide you with an unusual link back into your family's past.

Old photographs may show an ancestor wearing cufflinks to adorn shirtsleeves, the sleeves of frock coats or a dinner jacket. Check to see whether he favoured the fashionable 'kissing' cuffs (where the sleeve edges are just touching), barrel cuffs (where they are more sedately folded over), or 'dress sets', where a set of shirt studs matched exactly the design of the cufflinks themselves. Alternatively, your family cufflinks might still reside in the box in which they were bought – a clue to the whereabouts of a male relative or the person who bought them for him at a particular time.

Cufflinks are, of course, most useful to family history when there is paperwork connected with them; a letter or a will, for example, in which particular pieces are described and perhaps even valued. There might even be a family story that explains how certain cufflinks came into the possession of your great-grandfather or uncle. They were often given as gifts for weddings and – particularly – graduations. But even without this supporting evidence there are a number of ways in which the items themselves can point us to aspects of our ancestors' lives.

Sir Arthur Sullivan (1842–1900), one half of the duo Gilbert and Sullivan, joint creators of fourteen comic operas. A lifelong bachelor, Sullivan had many romantic affairs; he poses here in fashionable 'kissing cuffs'. (H.V. Morton, *Pageant of the Century*, 1934)

CUFFLINKS IN HISTORY

In the first place, inherited cufflinks might provide you with a taste of the era and social circumstances in which your ancestor lived.

The first 'cuff buttons' appeared in the seventeenth century. They were made of glass and linked with a chain. and they gradually replaced the ribbons or pieces of string that had traditionally been used to fasten cuffs. This coincided with a change in perceptions about men's clothing: shirts started to be considered an outer rather than an undergarment, and were on display rather than hidden away under other items of clothing. In the eighteenth century cufflinks were still seen as precious objects and remained the provenance of the very wealthy. They were handmade, and comprised gold or silver faces with precious jewels as decoration.

In the 1840s the 'French cuff' or 'double cuff' (a cuff that doubled back on itself) became stylish, and produced a higher demand for cufflinks. The middle classes started to wear cufflinks using cheaper materials such as gold-coloured alloys and fake diamonds. Many cufflinks were worn on top of the cuff (rather than at the side) so that they could be seen more clearly and could make a clear statement about the wealth and position of the man who wore them.

From the mid-nineteenth century cufflinks were becoming much more popular. A variety of fastening mechanisms were devised, with the most popular being those that had one decorative panel with a swivel-bar mechanism at the back to secure the cufflink in place once it had been pushed through the button holes. Many cufflinks of this period were very simple and business-like in design, reflecting a Victorian middle-class male culture of hard work and sobriety.

From 1860 new manufacturing techniques, particularly electroplating (which combined gold and silver with other metals), helped the large-scale manufacture and distribution of gold- and silver-plated cufflinks. Mourning cufflinks made from black jet were also very popular, particularly after the death of Prince Albert in 1861. Pearl and onyx cufflinks were also worn to signal bereavement, as were glass cufflinks that framed a lock of an ancestor's hair.

In 1862 cufflinks made an appearance at the Great World Exposition (or International Exhibition) in London. This show, which attracted over 6 million visitors over six months, displayed large inventions, such as machinery used in cotton mills, alongside smaller artistic developments such as rugs, silver and glassware. Cufflinks became part of the staple wardrobe of the middle-class Victorian man and some, no doubt, had great sentimental value. The superstitious Charles Dickens always wore the same pair of dented cufflinks for luck when he gave public readings.

Many cuffs were detachable. A man might wear the same shirt several times but he would change his cuffs every evening, to give the appearance of having a different (and clean) shirt. Button fastenings were unworkable on cuffs that had been starched stiff. This meant that cufflinks were essential, and were often worn with matching collar studs to go with detachable collars. The Parisian Boyer establishment was started in 1867, specialising in collar studs and removable shirt fronts. Cufflinks were created in mother-of-pearl, pearls, enamel, miniature mosaic work and precious or semi-precious stones. Tiffany, Cartier and Fabergé started to design different cufflinks to suit different occasions and mood. Some of these incorporated materials and themes that reflected Britain's empire.

In 1880 American George Kermentz began mass-producing single-sided cufflinks from a converted Civil War-era cartridge shell machine. This technology, combined with the earlier invention of electroplating, enabled yet cheaper cufflinks to be produced.

At the turn of the twentieth century cufflinks appeared with art nouveau motifs, including garlands, foliage and irises and the profiles of women. In 1904 the French shirtmaker Charvet started to make cufflinks from silk (also known as 'French knots', 'monkey's fists' or 'Turk's Heads'). At about the same time, clothing companies started mass-producing shirts that already had buttons attached to their cuffs, and consequently the trade in cufflinks declined somewhat. There was, however, a burgeoning trend in cufflinks with heraldic designs and mottos.

In the Edwardian period more women started to wear cufflinks to indicate their emancipation, their education and their desire to be treated equally with men. Such women were treated with suspicion for dressing in masculine fashions. Some were undoubtedly lesbians (or 'sexual inverts' as the terminology of the times would have them), who perhaps wore cufflinks as part of an unspoken declaration of their sexuality. The writer 'John' Radclyffe Hall (1880–1943) and her lover the sculptor and translator Una Troubridge (1887–1963) habitually dressed in a stylish masculine manner, donning shirts and cufflinks. On Hall's death in 1943 Troubridge adopted her 'poplin shirts, dressing gowns, cufflinks and jodhpurs'. Some years later Troubridge became fascinated with the (male) Italian opera singer Nicola Rossi-Lemeni, and as a mark of her appreciation gave him Hall's sapphire cufflinks.

Cufflinks from the 1920s are relatively easy to identify. The art deco movement gave rise to bold bright colours and abstract geometric motifs. Russian jewellery designers who had fled to America and Europe after the revolution in 1917 produced the most popular kind of cufflinks of this decade, made from a metal base covered with silica (i.e. enamel). Eventually Cartier, Chaumet, Mellerio and Boucheron also pursued the trade in enamel. Platinum and white gold cufflinks were also popular during the inter-war period.

Methods of fastening were changing alongside changes in design. In 1924 the Boyer establishment created the 'rolling button' or 'rod-type' cufflink, made up of a stud linked to a rod that swivelled along its whole length between two stems. And then in 1930 'press stud' or 'snap style' cufflinks came into fashion. These consisted of two identical studs, often in Bakelite, mother-of-pearl or enamel, which locked together via a small projection on one end and a matching depression on the other end.

From the 1930s to the 1950s, with a worsening economic climate, manufacturers turned to cheaper materials and novelty designs. Cufflinks were mass-produced in Catalin or Bakelite, plastic and gold plate. Many designs catered for the interests of 'typical' middle-class men: dogs, game birds, horses and golfers. The fashion for cufflinks declined in the 1960s with the arrival of ready-sewn plastic buttons on cuffs, and the fashion for wearing leisurewear rather than formal attire.

WHAT CUFFLINKS MIGHT TELL YOU ABOUT YOUR ANCESTOR

As well as alerting you to the historical period in which they were acquired, cufflinks may tell you something about your ancestor's class status. 'Double sided' ('double panelled' or 'double-faced') cufflinks are traditionally of the highest quality and may indicate the wealth or elevated social status of an ancestor. From the late nineteenth-century, 'single-faced' cufflinks (consisting of a one piece 'button-back' design, with decoration on the crown at one end and a smaller, plain metal head at the other) became popular with the masses. These, together with 'dumbbell' or 'shank-style' cufflinks (with a gently curved but rigid shank), which came to fashion in the early 1900s, may also denote an ancestor of lower social status. As a brief rule of thumb, the more difficult a cufflink is to fasten, the higher the class to which your ancestor probably belonged!

Cufflinks might also signal membership of an association. Some clubs, societies and military regiments issued cufflinks to their members. In 2008 a single cufflink dating back to the late eighteenth century was found in the mud on the banks of the River Thames. It was discovered that this was one of a limited number of such items that were presented to the officers serving Admiral Adam Duncan of Lundie to celebrate his victory at the Battle of Camperdown against the combined Dutch and French fleets on 11 October 1779. Be careful, however, of ascribing your cufflinks to one organisation or another; there are many modern novelty cufflinks with occupational or military themes.

Cufflinks may also tell you something about your ancestor's interests or character. The predilections of the owner of a pair of fox-head hunting horn cufflinks, for example, speak for themselves. A few rare examples may have messages engraved upon them that can give you an insight

Cufflinks by Tiffany: your family cufflinks might still reside in the box in which they were bought – a clue, perhaps, to the whereabouts of a male relative at a particular time. (Author's collection)

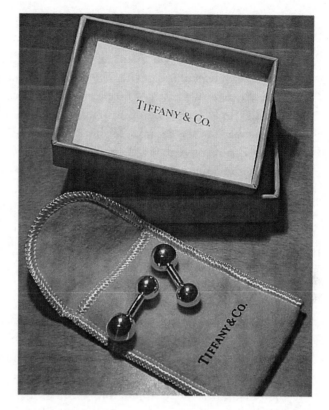

into the lives of their owner. In 1935 Wallis Simpson gave the soon-to-be Edward VIII a pair of platinum cufflinks set with diamonds, made by Cartier but designed by herself. On the back was the inscription 'Hold Tight', a reference to the difficulties that the two were facing in formalising their relationship in the face of public disapprobation. Edward, it seems, heeded the advice. He abdicated at the end of 1936, and seven months later he and Simpson were married.

Then there is the matter of the identity of the owner. In the late nineteenth century cufflinks became more personalised. Some were engraved with initials or dates, and these, of course, are a genealogist's delight. Monograms of men's names tend to have all the initials in the right order and at the same size. On some cufflinks the initials of the owner are on the reverse of the decorated face. Be careful, however, not to confuse monograms with the maker's mark, which may also be made up of initials.

CUFFLINKS ON THE *TITANIC*

One memorable historical event in which cufflinks made a notable appearance was the sinking of the *Titanic* in 1912. The magnificent vessel carried a clientele of wealthy European and American businessmen and their families. In its barber's shop passengers could purchase gold cufflinks made in the shape of the 'unsinkable' ship. Only one pair of these appears to have survived, now owned by a Belgian collector.

In the days following the tragedy, the bodies of 328 victims were picked up at the site of the sinking, and fatality reports were completed in order to aid later identification. These included a full description of the physical appearance of the bodies and of the personal effects found upon them. Clothing, jewellery and other belongings were placed in mortuary bags to be claimed by relatives. Many of the male passengers who had been travelling on first-class tickets were wearing cufflinks – an indisputable sign of their wealth and superior class status.

One of these men was Colonel John Jacob Astor, aged 47 – builder of the Astoria Hotel, New York, and the wealthiest victim of the tragedy. His body (number 124 to be pulled from the ocean) had upon it when found, among other personal effects, a gold watch, gold and diamond cufflinks and a diamond ring with three stones. Another first-class passenger, Alexander Oskar Holverson, aged 42 (body number 38) had gold mother-of-pearl cufflinks and studs to match. His pockets also contained a second pair of cufflinks (of a material not described), suggesting that he had gathered together his prized possessions before the ship sank. Yet another passenger, Irishman James Farrell, handed his cameo cufflinks to a woman, Katie Gilnagh, whose life he saved as she climbed into lifeboat 16. Farrell lost his life in the disaster. As a mark of her respect and gratitude to him, Miss Gilnagh posted the cufflinks back to his home in Ireland after the tragedy.

It is worth remembering that many of these cufflinks were extremely valuable. After the sinking one widow tried (unsuccessfully) to sue the shipping company, the White Star Line, for the price of her husband's effects, including his cufflinks. For these wealthy men cufflinks had been a key part of their small but expensive collection of personal jewellery, which also included fountain pens, tie clips, watches and rings made in similar materials. Tellingly, none of the unidentified bodies from the wreckage – those mainly of ordinary sailors, cooks and the like – were wearing cufflinks.

So intimately connected have cufflinks become with the memory of the tragedy that a centenary exhibition of rescued artefacts featured a single gold cufflink in a case — a poignant reminder of the end of one life and perhaps, too, of the end of an era of affluence and decadence never to reappear. A final rather ghoulish irony is that centenary souvenir cufflinks are today available for purchase, purportedly made from metal gleaned either from the wreck or from the Belfast boatyard where the ship was built.

Flamboyant or conservative, gadfly or company man — the chances are that you may glimpse your ancestor's personality in the cufflinks he left behind. At times in history when there were few other fashion accessories available by which a man could show his individuality, the diamond or decorated cufflink peeking out from his sleeve was a rare opportunity for self-expression.

FIND OUT MORE

Alan Flusser, *Dressing the Man: Mastering the Art of Permanent Fashion*, HarperCollins, 2002.

Susan Jonas and Marilyn Nissenson, *Cufflinks*, Harry N. Abrams, 1991.

Guy David Lambrechts, *Antique Cufflinks 1860–1960*, self-published, 2011.

Bertrand Pizzan and Jean-Noel Liaut, *Cufflinks*, Assouline, 2002.

antiquecufflinks.blogspot.com — for a gallery of interesting and unusual cufflinks in a variety of designs and from a variety of periods.

www.jewelryexpert.com/catalog/Antique-Cufflink-Archive.htm — compare your antique cufflinks with those in the archive.

www.blog.thecanadianencyclopedia.com/blog/posts/identifying-the-titanics-victims — details of the victims of the Titanic and their personal effects.

A Waft of History

PERFUME

How many of us have sniffed delightedly at an object inherited from an ancestor – the nutmeg and cinnamon scent of old books, the sweet and spicy smell inside an old wooden writing desk, or the camphor and cloves of a chest of old linen? Our sense of smell is one of the ways in which we fleetingly repossess the past and connect with the worlds of our ancestors. More evocative still than the smells of such everyday domestic items are the perfumes of earlier ages.

A waft of a favourite scent, the tang of hair oil or the zing of an aftershave can send us instantly spiralling backwards to those people with whom we shared our youth, or other significant events now quite distant in time. Many of us hold on to bottles of perfumes long after their 'best before' date as a reminder, visual and olfactory, of people and times that have gone by. The liquids may long since have oxidised and gone a

This scent bottle was made in 1924 and sold in the Co-op shortly before the common practice of buying perfume in a pharmacy and decanting it into bottles ended. (Beamish, The Living Museum of the North)

deep amber in colour, but if you have kept such an item of perfumery at the back of your bathroom cupboard, why not take it out and inhale its magic again. Surprisingly enough, it might just be able to tell you something about your family history.

SCENT AND MEMORY

Strange as it may seem, in family history research scent might prove a useful method of activating the memories of elderly relatives before conducting an oral interview. It is well known that prompts in the form of objects or photographs can certainly help the retrieval of information, but it might also be worth tuning into your subject's sense of smell. Researchers believe that smell leads to more emotional recollections and those that are further back in time than mere visual or verbal clues.

Relatives of those suffering from dementia or Alzheimer's are advised to bring scent prompts to meetings to aid recollection and conversation: perfume or cologne, freshly cut flowers or pot pourri, spices and herbs such as cinnamon and nutmeg, basil, lemon balm or chocolate. Some scents may remind people of certain times in their family history, or even particular (and complete) scenes. Vimto and corned beef have been known to revive memories of the Second World War; chalk and crayons of time spent as pupils or teachers. It seems that using a scent prompt can improve an interviewee's comprehension and recall, particularly of events long ago.

Recent research has also found that people born in different decades associate specific smells with their childhoods. Those born in the 1920s apparently remember their early years when presented with the natural smells of flowers, grass, rose, pine, soap and manure; people born in the 1930s reminisce to the scents of flowers, hay, sea air, pine and burning leaves; those born in the 1940s recall more manufactured scents, including baby powder and a mother's perfumes; 1950s' babies add a father's cologne, crayons, pine and play-doh to their list of scent triggers; and those born in the 1960s (less romantically) include chlorine, detergent and motor oil. Of course, relatives from other countries and cultures may respond to different scent stimuli, including the aromas of the traditional foods, flowers and remedies of their home countries.

There is science behind the connection between scent and memory. When you first perceive a scent you connect it to an event, person or thing.

When you smell the scent again it can trigger memory in the form of a conditioned response. This all happens because the olfactory bulb is part of the limbic system (the emotional centre of the brain), and it is connected particularly to two cerebral structures, the amygdala and the hippocampus, which also play an important part in the storing of memories. Indeed, among our five senses smell has the strongest and most direct connection to memory.

PERFUMES FOR WOMEN

In the eighteenth century wealthy women used perfumes that had been handmade from natural ingredients. Herbal scents (made from marjoram, thyme, clove and rosemary) were very popular. These continued in the nineteenth century but were joined by light and floral scents, including rose, jasmine, lavender and, the favourite, violet.

The perfumes worn by our early nineteenth-century female ancestors were probably not sprayed on the skin but rather used to scent gloves, handkerchiefs or other items of clothing. Perfumes helped to 'announce' women in society and to attract suitors. It was commonly held that 'respectable' women should only wear light, pure scents derived from a single garden flower, leaving the more complex and headier musks to those women of more dubious morals.

As in so many other spheres of life, science inevitably got mixed up with the business of perfume-making by the 1850s. Pharmacists were able to make perfume on their own premises using alcohol distilled from rice wine, malt liquor or brandy. They were free to use whatever names they wished, with the most popular appellations being 'Jockey Club', 'New Mown Hay' and 'Mille Fleurs' – names that must, at this time, have represented as many different fragrances as there were pharmacies making them.

George Dodd, a writer for *Household Words* magazine, was disgusted to find that many perfumes he had thought of as natural were in fact made by scientific processes, and wrote in October 1852:

Whether any perfumed lady would be disconcerted at learning the sources of her perfumes, each lady must decide for herself … [It has been found] that many of the scents said to be procured from flowers and fruits, are really produced from anything but flowery sources; the perfumers are chemists enough to know that similar odours may be often produced from dissimilar substances, and if the half-crown bottle of perfume really has the required odour, the perfumer does not expect to be asked what kind of odour was emitted by the substance whence the perfume was obtained ... Many a fair forehead is damped with eau de *millefleurs*, without knowing that its essential ingredient is derived from the drainage of cowhouses. The ... question is one of commercial honesty, in giving a name no longer applicable, and charging too highly for a cheaply produced scent. This mode of saving a penny is chemically right, but commercially wrong.

It was only towards the end of the nineteenth century that synthetic materials (primarily coal tar) started to be used in the manufacture of perfumes. The first of these was Fougère Royale by Paul Parquet for Houbigant in 1884. This used a synthetic molecule, coumarin, created by the British chemist William Henry Perkin in 1875. Coumarin, said to smell of new-mown hay, gave a long-lasting scent. The perfume also contained notes of oak moss and lavender.

In the late nineteenth century the range of fragrances available to perfumiers became much larger, and perfumes now came within the budget of many more women. Some of our late Victorian ancestors may have chosen their perfumes because they were worn by the famous women who were the heroines of the day. The actress Sarah Bernhardt, for example, notoriously wore Jicky by Guerlain and Quelques Fleurs L'Original by Houbigant. Lillie Langtry, Victorian mistress of the Prince of Wales, became associated with the distinctive mild, spicy, herbal fragrance of Pear's Soap after appearing in its advertising campaign. Another famous actress, Ellen Terry, became associated with the pure, clean scent of camellias.

In the early twentieth century the perfume industry burgeoned and became far more sophisticated. If our ancestors were not rich enough to keep up with all the changes in clothing fashion of their times, perfume was a cheaper way of staying *à la mode*. There were scents to be worn in the mornings, the afternoons or the evenings, perfumes to suit different age groups and even to reflect different moods. While many scents were available throughout the century some had their heyday in very specific eras – and may throw some light on the social history of the period in which they were bought and worn.

Soldiers returning from the First World War brought home French perfumes made by the manufacturer Coty for their loved ones. The enlightened women

"SHE CAUGHT SIGHT OF A SMELLING-BOTTLE ON THE CHIMNEY-PIECE."

Alongside their perfume bottles, female Victorian ancestors may also have carried small bottles of smelling salts (preparations of ammonium carbonate and perfume), which were used as a restorative to revive consciousness if they suffered a fainting fit. (*The Girl's Own Paper*, 1892)

of the 1920s, with their bobbed hair and short dresses, characteristically chose musky 'masculine' scents and wore them in the evenings. After the Second World War light, floral daytime perfumes, to match the new mood of celebration and optimism, were the scents of choice for the middle classes. In the 1950s far more people were able to afford perfumes such as those made by Revlon, Max Factor and Yardley's. Perfumes became available through more outlets and (importantly) in duty-free shops.

Many of our female ancestors will have worn a signature scent throughout their lives. A recent blogger recalls a moving experience after he accidentally encountered a whiff of the French perfume Arpège, launched in 1927. Suddenly and inexplicably he felt a 'nice, warm, reassuring and happy feeling' but couldn't think why. For the next few days he carried around various tester strips soaked in the fragrance. At last he remembered: his grandmother had worn Arpège. The memories clarified. He was transported back to the old lady's bedroom with its ornate dressing table and the bottle of Arpège with its gold stopper. He remembered watching his grandmother dabbing the perfume behind her ears and on her neck and wrists; he remembered her using her purse spray to scent the lining of her coat. It was a small step from this to remembering the names of his grandmother's siblings and the town of her birth.

PERFUMES FOR MEN

Eighteenth- and early nineteenth-century male aristocrats took perfumed baths and used 'Hungary' water (a mixture of herbs and alcohol), or rose water when shaving. A later development was eau-de-Cologne (a concoction of lemon, orange, bergamot, rosemary, bitter orange and neroli). Napoleon was well known for his exaggerated use of this 'aqua mirabilis' or 'wonder water', which he would pour liberally over his neck and head every time he washed. Other wealthy men used eau de Cologne on the flesh, on the clothes, as a mouthwash, and even swigged it as a cure for hangovers. But as the nineteenth century progressed the Victorians came to view the perfumed male with mistrust. As one writer, Edmund Saul Dixon, put it in 1857 in an article in *Household Worlds*:

> Perfumes are better altogether discarded by well-dressed gentlemen who are past the age of dandihood. Extreme personal cleanliness is the most judicious cosmetic we can use. Our money is more wisely laid out on Windsor soap and huckaback towels than on eau-de-Cologne and essence of millefleurs.

An English classic for men: lavender aftershave made by the company Potter & Moore, Mitcham, London (established 1749). (Author)

Men of the Victorian period were scented only indirectly through fragrant linen and hair oils, and masculine perfumes fell out of fashion. In the early years of the twentieth century our male ancestors are more likely to have smelt of 'tobacco, tweed and beer' than any manufactured fragrance. It was not until after the Second World War that perfumes for men reappeared in the form of aftershaves – toilet waters with a little antiseptic added. These were followed by talcum powders and then splash on eau-de-Colognes.

PERFUME BOTTLES

In the early Victorian period perfume was usually sold in plain bottles and then decanted into perfume bottles once the buyer got home. Many scent bottles from this period were made of coloured glass. In the second half of the nineteenth century silver scent bottles were popular, sometimes in combination with glass and ceramics. From 1842 manufacturers could register a design to protect it from imitations. Such bottles were marked with a diamond-shaped device, and from 1883 with a registration number. You can see the original drawings and a description of these at the National Archives in Kew.

The 1870s saw the discovery of so-called 'cameo glass', from which many perfume bottles came to be made. Many new designs came into being in the 1880s, and they had a variety of shapes from musical instruments to birds' eggs, shells, fruit and nuts. In the last decade of the nineteenth century, as the commercial perfume industry took off, designers, inspired by the art nouveau movement, also started to experiment with traditional packaging. At first this concentrated on the label and box, with many floral designs being employed.

In 1907 the French perfumier Coty asked René Lalique to design labels for scent bottles, and later the bottles themselves. Many of the bottles were decorated with nude or classically draped female figures. In the following two decades perfume bottles went through a period of imaginative and dramatic design. Lalique made bottles for many of the big perfumiers, including Guerlain, Houbigant, D'Orsay, Roger & Gallet, and Worth. From 1910 there was a particular fashion for oriental designs.

In the 1920s a number of fashion designers entered the perfume industry, and the packaging of perfume – taking on a number of themes from the art deco movement – became an even more important component of the consumer experience. Finally there was an end to the practice of decanting the perfume into the buyers' own bottles. Cosmetics and perfume became much more affordable and there was a huge increase in sales.

In the Depression of the 1930s some perfume companies closed down. Perfume bottles became less imaginative and were often made by machine. The scents inside them seemed to some less dramatic, and more comforting, warm and reassuring – an antidote, perhaps, to the uncertainty of the times. Floral designs on bottles and packaging became less popular and were replaced by bottles with more urban designs, some even inspired by Hollywood movies.

During the Second World War there were further changes in the perfume industry. Land was needed to grow food, and French manufacturers struggled to grow enough flowers for scent production. Fewer glass bottles were produced. There were also more powdered perfumes because of a scarcity of alcohol. In general, the perfume industry showed less creativity both in the scents themselves and in their presentation during the 1940s.

After the war the perfume industry was re-established and many new perfumers emerged, with Christian Dior and Nina Ricci both releasing perfumes that were highly original in scent and presentation. By the 1950s our ancestors were once again wearing perfume that was romantic and aspirational.

UNDERSTANDING YOUR ANCESTOR'S PERFUME

With a little knowledge about perfume and perfume bottles, a family story about perfume might be better interpreted. In February 1939 Mary Wilkinson, the 30-year-old wife of an engine driver, bought a bottle of perfume as a present for the midwife who had assisted her at home as she gave birth to her second child, a boy. Evening in Paris, a sweet, smooth, creamy and slightly wood-based scent was released in 1928 by Bourjois. A decade later it was affordable as a one-off special gift to those in the upper working classes, even those like Mary, living in small northern English towns. The dark blue phenolic perfume bottle had a gold label, looked appealing and came in a variety of different novelty shapes, including an owl and even a bedroom door.

Mary's choice of perfume perfectly sums her up. She had worked in a department store, which is probably where she first came across the scent. She was artistic, had social aspirations and no longer had to work. The gift of this perfume, in a bottle shaped like a top hat, to a woman of slightly lower status than herself, marked her sense of achievement at an important event. Mary must have been abreast of the trends. Evening in Paris went on to become a scent synonymous with the war years, as reminiscent of the early 1940s as nylon tights. By the 1950s it was being described as 'the perfume that more women wear than any other in the world'.

Today there are a number of websites that can help you to date your antique scent and its bottle. Be aware that some perfumes had an annual update. Magie by Lancome, for example, was released in 1950, but every Christmas there was a new version. A quick guide to the dates of release of the major perfume brands can be found at www.en.wikipedia.org/wiki/List_of_perfumes. To find out more about the composition and smell of your perfume, go to www.perfumeprojects.com/museum/Museum. For more of the fascinating social history behind many perfumes see www.perfumeshrine.blogspot.com or www.basenotes.net.

A few of the best-known fragrances of the twentieth century, with something of their historical context, are described below:

1905 L'Origon by Coty. A fragrance of iris and violet made using a combination of natural and synthetic ingredients. This was the first perfume to be marketed in an attractive bottle (with a gold label designed by Lalique) rather than in the traditional packaging of the apothecary's cask and leather box.

1921 Chanel No. 5 by Chanel. Coco Chanel once said that a woman 'should smell like a woman and not like a flower', and this best-selling fragrance aimed to achieve just that. It has a floral top note of ylang-ylang and neroli, with a heart of blends of jasmine and rose above a woody base of sandalwood and vetiver. The perfume was 'revolutionary' in scent and presentation. The elegant square bottle with bevelled edges aimed to make the perfume almost unisex – appealing to the more enlightened women of the times. During the 1930s lover and muse Laura Wishart sent writer Laurie Lee pound notes dabbed with Chanel No. 5 as inspiration for the cause for which he was fighting in the Spanish Civil War. Chanel bottles can be dated at chanelperfumebottles.webs.com/datingchanelbottles.htm.

1925 Shalimar by Guerlain. A feminine fragrance with iris, vanilla, and rose – inspired by the interest in the Orient that was sweeping Europe at the time. Its name came from the Shalimar gardens in which Shah Jahan was said to have wooed his great love Mumtaz before she died and he built her stunning mausoleum, the Taj Mahal. This perfume came in one of the most recognisable bottles of all time.

1932 Je Reviens by Worth. The name, meaning 'I will return', ensured that this was to become a popular gift from soldiers to their loved ones during the Second World War. The bottle, designed by Lalique, was a tall, ribbed bottle in dark blue glass resembling New York skyscrapers. It had a sky blue stopper and came in a box covered in chrome.

1935 Joy by Jean Patou. A concoction of roses and jasmine flowers, this was the most expensive scent of its times and voted the scent of the twentieth century at the Fragrance Foundation FiFi awards, 2000.

1938 Old Spice by Shulton. The first spicy oriental fragrance for men.

1944 Femme by Rochas. The first spicy, fruity fragrance for women packaged in an attractive bottle inspired by the shape of a woman's body. It was at first sold as a limited edition to subscribers only, because of war shortages.

1947 Miss Dior by Dior. A light, fresh, daytime perfume aimed at the debutantes 'coming out' in the first years after the Second World War. This was presented in an elegant clear crystal Baccarat bottle, appearing classic and luxurious.

1948 L'Air du Temps by Nina Ricci. This came in a bottle shaped like a sunburst, with a stopper decorated with a dove (designed to celebrate the post-war peace). Correspondingly, the lid of the box was lined with white silk and depicted a woman and a flying dove. The box for this perfume in 1951 was in the shape of a birdcage covered in yellow silk, which could be illuminated by a battery.

1953 Youth Dew by Estée Lauder. Hailed as one of the sexiest perfumes ever, it was also one of the first perfumes that women went out and bought for themselves – partly because it was also packaged as a bath oil.

1955 Intimate by Revlon. A 'friendly' perfume with mass-market appeal and a cheaper price tag than many of its contemporaries.

1958 Hypnotique by Max Factor. The marketing for this perfume was noticeably sexual for the times. Featuring a vamp-like woman mesmerising and seducing her man with the fragrance, it tied in with the themes of change and emancipation for women that characterised the feminist movement of the 1960s.

You will find a great deal more information about these perfumes and many others on the Internet. Often they are accompanied by nostalgic reminiscences of times and relatives lost. So when quizzing elderly family members about their history remember that where a photograph of someone might elicit nothing but a name, the same prompt, together with a whiff of great-grandmother's perfume, or less glamorously cigarette smoke or cod liver oil, might bring back a whole host of useful memories.

FIND OUT MORE

Jim Drobnick, *The Smell-Culture Reader*, Berg, 2006.

Ken Leach, *Perfume Presentation, 100 Years of Artistry*, KRES publishing, 1997.

Annick Le Guerer, *Scent: The Mysterious and Essential Powers of Smell*, Random House, 1992.

Alexandra Walker, *Scent Bottles*, Shire, 2002.

www.basenotes.net/content – an independent online guide to thousands of fragrances.

www.perfumebottles.org – for collectors of perfume bottles.

www.fashion-era.com/perfume_history – timeline of perfumes throughout recent history.

www.perfume2000.com/History – a detailed history of some of the world's greatest perfumes.

www.harrismuseum.org.uk – the Harris Museum and Art Gallery, Preston, where the largest scent bottle collection in Britain (the Mrs French Collection) can be viewed.

www.perfumes.com/eng/bottles – on the dating of perfume bottles.

13

Floral Tributes

FLOWERS

Flowers have always been called upon in the celebration of the key events in family history – courtships, marriages, births and deaths. There are many different ways in which you may come across them in the course of your family history research.

FLOWERS IN PHOTOGRAPHS

You may find flowers used as a prop in Victorian photography. From the 1870s photographers used painted backdrops to suggest that their sitters were outside, and all sorts of flora and foliage were brought into the studio to enhance that effect. Additionally, your ancestors may have worn flowers in their hair or their buttonholes in a photograph. Charles Dickens wore his favourite flower, a red geranium, in his buttonhole at all his public readings to symbolise his 'gentility', and it is just possible that your ancestor may have worn or carried a particular kind of bloom to convey a special meaning of some sort or other. There is more on the Victorian language of flowers below.

More likely, baskets of flowers will be held by young children or single blooms worn in the hair of older girls as a generally understood symbol of their purity and innocence. Victorian women and children were often depicted close to or at one with nature, in a deliberate move to disassociate them from the sullied public world of commerce. Julia Margaret Cameron (1815–79), a late Victorian photographer primarily of women and children, was particularly fond of incorporating flowers into her photographs, both as symbols of the beauty and purity of her sitters (roses and lilies were a favourite) and to aid the artistic composition. By the 1890s the photographic studio often looked like a conservatory, complete with palms and exotic blooms.

Flowers in photographs may also help you to understand what occasion is being celebrated. In the late nineteenth century couples who had just been married often proceeded straight from the church to a photographer's studio. Since many brides did not wear a wedding dress as we know it, but simply their best dress, wedding photographs may sometimes only be identified as such by the fact that the man is wearing a buttonhole or the woman carrying flowers. Wedding anniversaries in the twentieth century were traditionally associated with certain kinds of flower, which may appear in photographs of these occasions: from carnations given after one year, to daffodils after ten, asters after twenty, irises after twenty-five, lilies after thirty, gladioli after forty and lilies and violets after fifty. Look out for photographs in which women are carrying small bouquets of lilies or forget-me-nots. These may indicate that they are in mourning. A corsage of scabious indicates recent widowhood. If a person is surrounded by flowers, this may be an indication that this is a post-mortem photograph.

REAL FLOWERS

You may also come across real pressed flowers among family memorabilia, perhaps between the pages of an old book or family Bible. If you are very lucky these may have been labelled with names and dates. Sometimes flowers from wedding bouquets or funeral wreaths were saved. At other times pressed flowers paid tribute to a courtship, a friendship or simply a happy day spent somewhere. The most common kind of preserved flowers in the Victorian period were pansies, daisies, bluebells and violets, since these had the single layer of petals that were more successfully pressed.

Some Victorian women had small hand-held flower presses in which they preserved flowers between sheets of blotting paper. Presses might have an iron top held in place by a crank-like handle; others were bound with leather straps. Botany was an acceptable habit for a Victorian girl, although the reproductive habits of plants were usually sparingly taught! Dried and pressed flowers might be laid on velvet, silk or lace and then covered with glass and displayed as pictures, or converted into flower screens. Flower books or 'Herbariums' included preserved flowers, a little botanical detail and the occasional romantic verse. The nineteenth-century musician Clara Schumann (1819–96) kept a diary from 1857 to 1859 after the death of her husband, the composer Robert Schumann (1810–56), in which she pressed flowers and ferns and recorded details of the places she had been and the people she had been with on the days she collected them, for example, 'Souvenir of the Rhein, 1857, given to me in the summer by Johannes'.

The practice of keeping flowers associated with particular memories persisted well into the twentieth century, with many people treasuring blooms that reminded them of certain people or special occasions among their personal effects. Archived memorabilia belonging to the writer and feminist Vera Brittain (1893–1970) includes 'a pressed rose' from her friend the writer Winifred Holtby (1898–1935), dated 13 June 1935, 'Broom, from the Argonne Front, April 1936' and 'pressed flowers from Winifred Holtby's grave. July 19, 1938'.

A particularly significant flower, a poppy, was picked and preserved by Cecil Roughton, a 17-year-old soldier who served in the trenches of northern France in the First World War. A few years later he sent it home to his family with a note that read, 'Souvenir from a front line trench near Arras May 1916. C. Roughton 1923.' The poppy survives and has recently appeared in an exhibition of wartime art.

COURTSHIP

In 1850 Elizabeth Barrett Browning's *Sonnets from the Portuguese* described how her husband, the poet Robert Browning, had bombarded her with flowers during their courtship:

> Beloved, thou hast brought me many flowers
> Plucked in the garden, all the summer through,
> And winter, and it seemed as if they grew
> In this close room, nor missed the sun and showers.

Browning's gifts demonstrated to excess the Victorian practice of presenting an intended with floral bouquets at the beginning of a courtship. This was often a selection of herbs surrounding a flower or flowers, all chosen for their meanings. Indeed, throughout the betrothal process Victorian lovers might send hidden messages to each other by way of flowers. Of course, few of our ordinary Victorian ancestors would have been experts in the language of flowers, but some symbols would have been widely understood. Marigolds (or *calendula*), for example, symbolised sorrow and despair, but by adding a poppy, symbol of consolation, to the bouquet, the sender of flowers might suggest that he could soothe his lover's grief.

The association between flowers and emotions was age-old, but by the end of the nineteenth century it had developed into 'floriography', a complex language of flowers. This might be of interest to you as you research your family if you have inherited heirlooms decorated with flowers, which might have been given as gifts between lovers: items of jewellery, embroidered clothing, ornaments and the like. Beware, however: dozens of dictionaries of floriography were published in the nineteenth century, and they don't necessarily agree with each other about the meanings of certain flowers! The following is a selective list taken from the popular *Sunlight Year Book* of 1898:

Hollyhocks, originally from the East, were a favourite flower of the Victorians and symbolised ambition and fertility, qualities that make this picture of a young girl festooned with them rather suggestive and daring. (*The Girl's Own Paper*, 1886)

Acacia – Pure love
Bachelor's Buttons – Celibacy
Carnation (red) – Alas for my poor heart
Daisy – Innocence
Everlastings – Unending remembrance
Foxglove – An insecure acquaintance
Geranium (red) – Consolation
Hazel – Reconciliation
Ivy – Fidelity
Jasmine (white) – Amiability
Lavender – Distrust
Myrtle – Love
Orange Blossom – Purity
Peony – Shame
Quaking Grass – Agitation
Rose (yellow) – Jealousy
Snowdrop – Hope
Tulip (red) – Declaration of love
Violet – Faithfulness
Willow – Mourning

WEDDINGS

The legal and religious union of a man and a woman throughout history has rarely gone ahead without the accompaniment of a profusion of colourful and sweet-smelling symbols of joy and fertility. Bouquets of flowers, known as poseys, nosegays or 'tussie-mussies', have been carried by flower girls at weddings for centuries. And until modern times the choices of flowers in these and the bridal bouquet have depended far more on the symbolic meaning of the flowers involved than on their shape and colour.

Some of the symbolic meanings of flowers called upon at our ancestors' weddings were of ancient pagan origin, some had significant Christian meanings and still others took on meanings that were of particular importance to our society at a particular time. At some nineteenth-century weddings the subtlety of the flower arrangements was quite breathtaking: flowers could, for example, take on different meanings depending on whether they were placed in the cleavage, in the hair or over the heart.

Sometimes a collection of different flowers were chosen for the messages spelt out by their first letters: **L**ilac, **O**range Blossom, **V**iolet and **E**uphorbia, for example.

Regency bridal bouquets, such as those that would have been carried by Jane Austen's heroines, included flowers such as roses (love), peonies (riches and honour), sweet peas (blissful pleasure), lilies (life) and delphinium (levity), as well as herbs such as sage, which were thought to ward off bad luck, evil spirits and poor health. Greenery, such as ivy (the Christian symbol of eternal life) or thistle (symbol of protection), was also included. Sprigs from the bouquets were sometimes planted by the bridesmaids at the home of the bride and groom after the wedding to ensure marital contentment. If the sprigs took root quickly and bore bushes it was deemed likely that the bridesmaids themselves would soon marry,

Wedding of milkman Eddie Rollinson and Alice (maiden name unknown), late 1920s. Light-coloured arum and calla lilies, together with roses, were a favourite in the great armfuls of flowers that constituted 1920s bridal bouquets. For weddings on a budget, like this one, carnations were the order of the day. (Author's collection)

The type and number of bouquets in evidence in a group wedding photograph will give you some evidence of your ancestors' wealth and social status – or at least of the economic prosperity of the times. Look out for the bridal bouquets in photographs of weddings that took place in your family in the Victorian period. They often included rosemary (an ancient symbol of faithfulness) and orange blossom (a symbol of chastity). In 2011 Kate Middleton followed royal tradition by including a sprig of myrtle from the bush in Queen Victoria's personal garden at Osborne House on the Isle of Wight in her wedding bouquet. The myrtle (a star-like flower with creamy white petals and dark green leaves) traditionally symbolised love, affection, joy and happiness. It has graced all the important royal bridal bouquets from the mid-nineteenth century onwards. By the Victorian period myrtle had additionally come to symbolise duty, affection, discipline and home – the true values of Victorian womanhood. In the 1940s, an era of austerity, bridal bouquets – particularly those arranged in haste when a serviceman was on leave – were characteristically small and unostentatious, with flowers such as chrysanthemums plucked from the bride's garden sometimes being used.

BIRTHS

Your family birth certificates may remind you that in the late nineteenth and early twentieth centuries some of the older, more traditional names for girls (such as Anne, Jane and Elizabeth) were dropped in favour of what must have appeared the more fashionable flower names. Violet, for instance, came into vogue in the last two decades of the reign of Queen Victoria; there are two famous examples in the politician Violet Bonham-Carter (1887–1969) and the writer Violet Needham (1876–1967). Daisy was a common nickname for Margaret at the end of the nineteenth century (the French flower being known as a Marguerite). The name Iris (as in the writer Iris Murdoch (1919–99) was particularly popular in Britain between 1900 and 1920.

Whatever your ancestor's name, flowers (or gifts bearing pictures of flowers) have traditionally been given at the birth of a baby and at his or her christening to celebrate new life. Flowers at births and baptisms (which may appear in family photographs or on christening gifts of one sort or another) have been associated with distinct months of the year:

January – carnation
February – violet
March – daffodil
April – dahlia and sweet pea
May – lily of the valley and sunflower
June – honeysuckle and rose
July – larkspur
August – lily and gladiolus
September – forget-me-not and aster
October – calendula, rose and camellia
November – chrysanthemum
December – holly and narcissus

DEATHS

Symbols of the brevity and the transiency of life, flowers have long played a part at funerals. Traditionally they even had a practical purpose, to offset the smell of the decomposing body. In the distant past, churches were filled with flowers on religious occasions, but the Reformation put paid to this and Protestant churches were without flowers until they were reintroduced at the end of the nineteenth century. Whilst few objects found their way inside Christian coffins in the nineteenth century, flowers sometimes did so. In *Jane Eyre* (1848), Charlotte Brontë wrote that the coffins of the girls who died at Lowood School were filled with 'herbs and blossoms'.

In rural parishes your ancestors' graves may have been covered with fresh flowers around Easter. Here is how the Rev. Francis Kilvert (1840–79) wrote about this practice in his diary of 1870: 'As I walked down the Churchyard alone the decked graves had a strange effect in the moonlight and looked as if the people had laid down to sleep for the night out of doors, ready dressed to rise early on Easter morning.'

In more recent times floral tributes presented by grieving relatives at funerals have been recorded in newspaper obituaries. Old newspapers can now be searched by date and keyword in the libraries of the town in which the death was reported, or in some cases for a fee as scanned pages on various Internet sites including the British Newspaper Archive, www.britishnewspaperarchive.co.uk, and www.findmypast.com. Lists of bouquets and wreaths, together with the names, hometowns and in some cases, the relationships, of those donating, can make fascinating reading for family historians. In the *Gloucestershire Echo* of Thursday 15 August 1940, for example, the funeral is reported of Mr F.R. March, aged 24, a teacher and member of the Devonshire Regiment who had been killed while on active service. The list of floral tributes for this man is extensive and gives a great deal of information potentially useful to a genealogist, including names and relationships, addresses, and institutions to which he belonged, as well as giving a vivid description of the shapes and colours of his funeral:

Cross from his sorrowing mother, heart from Margaret [identified earlier in the obituary as a chief mourner and his fiancée], wreaths from dad, Auntie Lottie and Clara … St Gregory's Athletic Club ('to our beloved captian and thorough sportsman with sympathy and regret,') From the Commanding Officer, Officers, Warrant Officers, and NCOs of his battalion, the Devonshire Regiment; Intelligence Section; His Company of the Battallion of the Devonshire Regiment (in regimental colours) … All at 3 Alwyne Street, Birmingham … Flos [Flowers] Dorren, Wallis, Winnie and Arthur (Cousins) In addition to a wreath, the Regiment sent a beautiful vase for the grave.

From the late Victorian period flowers and foliage have appeared on memorial carvings alongside poignant personalised inscriptions. Lilies are very popular motifs on headstones, symbolising the restored innocence of the soul at death. Other common flowers and greenery used in memorial carvings are the passion flower (symbolising the Passion of Christ), roses (love),

The obituary of Mr F.R. Marsh, together with a full list of floral tributes, *Gloucestershire Echo*, 15 August 1940. (www. findmypast.co.uk)

FUNERAL OF MR. F. R. MARCH

MILITARY HONOURS FOR SPORTSMAN

The funeral took place on Tuesday of Mr. F. R. March, late of 24, Cleeve View-road, Cheltenham, who died while on active service with the Devonshire Regiment.

Mr. March, who was 24 and a member of the teaching staff of St. Gregory's Athletic Club, and formerly held the quarter-mile championship of both Gloucestershire and the Midland Counties.

The service took place at St. Stephen's Church and was conducted by the Rev. R. H. Sutch (Vicar), and Canon P. M. C. Johnstone (Vicar of All Saints').

The hymns, "Abide with Me," and "Nearer my God to Thee," and the Psalm, "The Lord is my Shepherd," were sung.

After the service, the cortege left the church for Sea Mills, Bristol, where the coffin was met by the military and interred at St. Mary's, Redcliff, Cemetery with full military honours.

The chief mourners were Mr. and Mrs. A. J. March (mother and father); Miss Margaret Whalley (fiance); Mr. and Mrs. B. Teague (uncle and auntie); Mr. and Mrs. H. Teague (uncle and auntie); Mrs. A. Read (auntie); Norman (cousin); Mr. Larry Cummins (St. Gregory's Athletic Club); Mr. G. Pardington (also representing the Headmaster, Mr. N. C. H. Edwards), Mr. George Houghton and Mr. Ray Sims, and other members of the staff of All Saints' School; Miss Grace Davis (School of Shorthand).

There were also many personal friends and representatives of various sporting and social bodies.

FLORAL TRIBUTES

The many beautiful floral tributes included: — Cross (from his sorrowing mother); Heart (from Margaret); Wreaths from Dad, Auntie Lottie, and Clara; Auntie Vi and Uncle Bert; Uncle Harry and Auntie Gertie; Cousin Norman; Auntie Flo, Arthur and family; Pamela (a pupil); Staff and Scholars (All Saints' School); All Saints' Old Boys' Association; Cheltenham and County Harriers; Ken; Ray; G. Houghton; Jack Blake and Hilda; Phillip and Mollie; Major Harford; K. Morris; Ida and Janet; Marling, Zetland, and Winscombe; Cheltenham Teachers' Association; St. Gregory's Athletic Club (to our beloved captain and thorough sportsman, with sympathy and regret); From all at Montague; Mr. and Mrs. Hodges and Hazel; Mr. and Mrs. Scott; Mrs Smith and family; Margaret's Mother and Dad; Mr. and Mrs. Mercer, Burnley; All at 3, Alwyn-street, Birmingham; Flos Doreen, Wallis, Winnie, and Arthur (cousins); One of Billy's friends; From the Commanding Officer, Officers, Warrant Officers, N.C.O.'s and men of his Battalion, the Devonshire Regiment; Intelligence Section; His Company of the Battalion of the Devonshire Regiment (in regimental colours); Sister Olga; Cheltenham Association Football League; Peter, Wife, and family, St. James-square; A Sincere Friend; Mrs. Balch and family; Pupils of the Shorthand School; Mr. and Mrs. Nellson.

In addition to a wreath, the Regiment sent a beautiful vase for the grave.

and ivy (symbolising eternal life). Sometimes flowers on memorial carvings are depicted with the stem broken to represent a life cut short.

FLOWERS AT HOME

Flowers dominated the Victorian home in all sorts of ways. Home decorations from wallpaper to cloth design were festooned with blooms. Jewellery, clothing and all manner of objects were fashioned from or decorated with flowers. Bunches of dried lavender scented drawers and wardrobes. Other flowers were employed in the kitchen, and your ancestor's handwritten recipe books may contain some surprises: crystallised or 'candied' violets (dipped in egg white and sugar) were used to decorate Victorian desserts in wealthy households; primroses, borage and nasturtiums appeared in salads; and marigolds were used in soup by the poor as an alternative to saffron. Other flowers were used as primitive medicines. Those who could not afford expensive pharmaceuticals may have resorted to the hedgerow in the treatment of family ailments: hyacinth bulbs, for example, were used in the treatment of diphtheria in the late nineteenth century, and lavender was used to treat indigestion, headaches and respiratory problems.

It was the duty of every middle-class housewife of the Victorian era to provide a happy, healthy and aesthetically pleasing home. The variety and splendour of flower decorations in an individual house said a lot about the wealth, social standing and taste of particular families, and flower arrangement was one of the few practical tasks that the middle-class housewife usually did not leave to the servants.

Advice writers went to great lengths in instructing women what to do with the blooms at their disposal, though the choice of flowers was, of course, more limited than it is now, and exotic flowers could only be grown by those who could afford hothouses. In the month of May 1892 *The Girl's Own Paper* – a popular magazine for young women – suggested the following complicated domestic flower decorations for the table:

> For a dinner party this month, make a bank of ivy down the middle of the table, using thick bushy pieces to raise it in the centre, and trails of the smaller kind to fringe the edge, these coming nearly to the line of the wineglasses, and at the corners right to the edge of the table, winding round any small dishes of olives or sweets which may be needed. [Include also] six white china

vases, containing each a well-grown head of lemon colour or terra-cotta azalea, with some light sprays of very vivid green asparagus or young fern.

Whether you are lucky enough to have inherited a description of your ancestor's festive drawing room, the preserved flowers of your grandmother's bridal bouquet, or a photograph of your great-aunt wearing an unusual corsage, spare a thought for the significance they might once have had.

FIND OUT MORE

Marina Heilmeyer, *The Language of Flowers: Symbols and Myths*, Prestel, 2001.
Geraldine Adamich Laufer, *Tussie-Mussies, the Victorian Art of Expressing Yourself in the Language of Flowers*, Workman Publishing, 1993.
Sandy Puckett, *Fragile Beauty: The Victorian Art of Pressed Flowers*, Warner, 1992.
Bobby J.A. Ward, *A Contemplation Upon Flowers: Garden Plants in Myth and Literature*, Timber, 2005.
www.buzzle.com/articles/list-of-flower-names-and-meanings-of-flowers.html – flowers and their meanings.
www.felbridge.org.uk/index.php?p=2_48 – descriptions of headstones, among them many floral ones, in the cemetery of St John the Divine, Felbridge.
www.weddingguideuk.com/articles/planning/chooseflowers.asp – some facts about wedding bouquets throughout history.

14

Like a Member of the Family

DOGS

A dog in an old family photograph always provides a talking point: the Great Dane stretched at the feet of its master; the red setter artistically seated next to a little girl with curls; a poodle snuggled up on great-grandmother's knee. Whatever else is being portrayed, dogs and other animals subtly alter the composition and dynamics of a photograph, bringing out the feelings and personality of the sitters in ways that would be impossible without them.

A BRIEF HISTORY OF OUR ANCESTORS AND THEIR DOGS

Dogs provided our ancestors of all classes with company, comfort, sport and livelihood. Throughout history it is said that in country parishes they were often taken along to church to keep the feet of their owners warm during the service! For centuries the wealthy had kept dogs primarily to guard their properties, but by the eighteenth century some types of dog, such as the spotted Dalmatian, were being bred among the aristocracy for their ornamental appearance.

As many poorer people moved into the cities from the countryside during the Industrial Revolution (1780–1850) they took with them their dogs, and several urban sports involving canines sprang up. Dog baiting survived even after other blood sports involving animals had been outlawed by the Cruelty to Animals Act (the first British law to tackle the welfare of animals) in 1835. At the same time many dogs throughout history were kept by men of the lower classes (such as shepherds, huntsmen and those in the military or police forces) as working animals.

It was only in the Victorian era that keeping dogs primarily as pets became popular among the middle classes. Cats too became part of the household, after a long history of being kept outside the domestic environment as utilitarian animals useful for catching rats and mice in barns and cellars. The constant self-grooming of cats appealed to middle-class Victorians, who regarded felines as very clean animals and as such an emblem of improved domestic hygiene during the period.

In the last decades of the nineteenth century dogs and cats achieved a status in British society that they held nowhere else in the world. Increased leisure time among the middle classes fostered an appetite for exhibitions, and in 1859 the first organised dog show was held, in Newcastle-upon-Tyne. The first National Cat Club show was held at Crystal Palace in 1887; 323 cats were entered. The British concern for animal welfare was illustrated by the founding of the Temporary Home for Lost and Starving Dogs, now Battersea Dogs and Cats Home, in Holloway by Miss Mary Tealby in 1860. Breed standards, written descriptions of each type of dog's appearance, movement and temperament, were put together by the Kennel Club (founded in 1873) and other hobbyist organisations, and in 1886 Crufts held its first dog show. The National Cat Club was founded in 1887 by Mr Harrison Weir.

DOGS IN THE RECORDS

Perhaps surprisingly dogs appear in all manner of records that might be of interest to a family historian. You will find fewer records relating to cats, but they appeared on innumerable objects as decoration during the Victorian period and beyond.

PAINTINGS

Wealthy ancestors who could afford to have portraits painted of themselves were also the ones who had portraits painted of their animals. A fashion for having one's dogs painted began after 1836, when the artist Edwin Landseer was commissioned to paint Princess (later Queen) Victoria's dog Dash, a Cavalier King Charles spaniel, for her seventeenth birthday. Landseer himself popularised Newfoundland dogs – celebrating them as rescue dogs with paintings such as *Off to the Rescue* (1827), *A Distinguished Member of the Humane Society* (1838) and *Saved* (1856). For more information about your ancestral dog painting see the reference work by William Secord, *Dog Painting: The European Breeds* (2000), which looks at the work of all the well-known nineteenth-century artists working in this genre.

PHOTOGRAPHS

In the past, as today, dogs were often considered as important members of the family, sharing in festivities such as birthdays, weddings and holidays – indeed, all the occasions upon which a photograph might have been taken. Because of this the presence of a dog before the camera may help you to discover quite a lot about your family history.

The long exposure times required of very early photography required subjects to keep still for a few minutes at a time. This was obviously not conducive to the portrayal of animals, but from the 1860s onwards (with the advent of shorter exposure times) pets of all kinds made more of an appearance before the lens. Pet portraits, on *cartes de visite* or the slightly larger cabinet cards, in which pets might appear alone, were popular from 1860, but more often an animal was seated next to a man, woman or child. Cats are less common in Victorian photographs than dogs, but they do make an occasional appearance. A Brighton photographer, Harry Pointer (1822–89), was well known for taking photographs of cats in amusing poses, which he presented in the *cartes de visite* format complete with amusing captions. By 1884 he had published about 200 different pictures, and these became known as the Brighton Cats series. You can see a good selection of these at: www.photohistory-sussex.co.uk/BTNPointerCats.htm.

Dogs in photographs can tell you something about your family's wealth and status in the past. For centuries dogs were popular with aristocratic families and not so much with people in the middle ranks of society, but from the Victorian period onwards more and more middle-class people started to keep pets. In 1897 the cost of a dog licence was 7s 6d – not an insubstantial amount at the time – and so having a dog or dogs quickly became one of the many outward signs that a family had 'made it'. Indeed, the very type of dog owned by middle- and upper-class families was increasingly viewed as a barometer of how fashionable they were – functioning in much the same way as a new hat or the length of a hemline.

Look out for certain types of small dog in the laps of your great aunts and other female relatives. Some of these animals were the runts of litters picked out as playthings for women and children. 'Toys', as they were known, went in and out of fashion, thus their presence in a photograph might help you to date it. At the beginning of the Victorian period, for example, popular dogs such as King Charles spaniels were cross-bred with Asiatic breeds to produce supposedly more attractive 'pug' dogs with short muzzles. In the 1890s a favourite miniature dog in London was a small Belgian breed – the Schipperke – mainly because its hair was short and black. Long-haired and white dogs tended to be less popular because they left visible hairs on furniture and gowns. The Sealyham terrier – a short white dog bred by crossing corgis with various breeds of terrier – was not officially recognised until 1910. About 2,000 such dogs were licensed in the 1920s, and the breed was made popular later in the twentieth century by glamorous women such as Princess Margaret. You are unlikely to see a Sealyham in a recent

(Probably) Mildred Hughes (aged about 6) and her curly-coated retriever, York, mid-1870s. (With thanks to Mary and Sandra Jeffrey)

photograph, however; in 2008 it was estimated that there were only forty-three left in Britain.

And, of course, there are dogs that have become extinct. The Norfolk spaniel and the English water spaniel had virtually disappeared by the beginning of the twentieth century, with an example of the latter last being spotted in 1930. Other dogs were bred for specific reasons at certain points in the past. Take the golden retriever, for instance. Any photograph featuring one of these has to have been taken after 1862 – and probably somewhat later. Improvements in firearms in the mid-Victorian period meant that more game was being shot by huntsmen on increasingly difficult terrain. Sir Dudley Marjoribanks, a Scottish gentleman, wanted to breed a dog that would be a good retriever of such birds but that would also be gentle and trainable. To this end, in 1862 he crossed a male yellow-coloured retriever, Nous, with a female Tweed water spaniel, Belle. The result was the golden retriever – a dog that was to become one of the great British favourites.

Dogs in photographs might also tell you more about what your ancestor did for a living. If a dog is portrayed with an adult male in a photograph, this might indicate – in the same way as the presence of an apron or a knife – that he was a tradesman, such as a butcher or baker. Look out for dogs that might reveal family employment as shepherds, huntsmen, ghillies or members of the military and police forces. From 1931 dogs may also appear in photographs as guide dogs for the blind.

THE CENSUS

Early censuses between 1801 and 1831 were just a headcount of the population and not properly standardised. Some of the enumerators appointed to carry out these censuses, such as local clergymen, went above and beyond the call of duty. The 1821 census for Hendon, London, for example, includes a count of the number of windows and the number of dogs present in each household. Enumerators for these early censuses were not asked to compile information on individuals, though some names of the heads of households were recorded. It is thus possible, if you know an ancestor's address, that you will be able to find out how many dogs a household had, even if you can't find out the names of the children. The early censuses are not available on the usual family history websites, but some of the returns can be viewed in local archives (the Hendon one is at Barnet Archives, London), and some local family history societies have made them available on CD Rom.

In later years some dogs got into the censuses by accident rather than by design. In 1911 the famous music hall artist named The Great Lafayette (living in the registration district of St Giles and Bloomsbury, London) entered his details on the census, stating that he had a 16-year-old 'daughter' named Beauty. The suspicions of the census enumerator were aroused and a red line was later scored through the entry. Beauty was in fact Lafayette's dog – a much-adored gift to him from the escapologist Harry Houdini. Lafayette was a master illusionist, rejoicing in the absurd, but Beauty was by no means the only family pet to enter the census records in this way. That same year a more ordinary family from Dublin, the Cullens, recorded, in addition to their six children, an unidentified family member named Tatters, aged 3. Again, the enumerator spotted the joke and tried to delete the entry.

Dogs also appear in the censuses indirectly through the occupations of ancestors: dog catchers, dog killers (employed by the parish to do away with stray dogs), dog groomers, dog wardens, dog-muzzle makers and dog breakers (trainers), to name but a few.

The presence of a dog on a family photograph might help you to date it. By the end of the Victorian period, there was a demand for particular types of miniature dog among the upper and middle classes. (Author's collection)

LICENCES

A dog licence found among family papers might give you the address of your ancestor at a particular time. Such a document from 1906 may be viewed at www.bbc.co.uk/ahistoryoftheworld/objects/t2wGbnUISCmq9FW1X_RoaQ. Dog licences were finally abolished in 1987.

COURT RECORDS

If you are searching court records that relate to an ancestor, don't be surprised if from 1871 you find him or her apprehended for a crime involving a dog. The Dogs Act of that year meant that more people were fined for not keeping their dogs properly under control. Dogs deemed particularly dangerous could be removed from their owners' possession and put down. In addition, the police had the power to detain, sell or destroy all stray dogs. Owners of dogs were responsible for any injury done by their dogs to sheep or cattle. Conversely, killing or wounding dogs also became a criminal offence. For more on how to find court records relating to an ancestor see www.nationalarchives.gov.uk/records/research-guides/crime-and-law.htm.

PET GRAVESTONES AND PET CEMETERIES

As honorary members of the family, dogs and cats were often buried on family property. The grounds of stately homes, such as Tatton Hall in Cheshire, shelter gravestones to canine friends. In the grounds of the home of actress Lily Langtry (1853–1929) in Kentford, near Newmarket, there is a grave to the dog Caesar, given to her by Queen Alexandra – an unusual gift, perhaps, since Langtry was well known to have had an affair with Alexandra's husband, Edward VII. There are also some examples here and there in ordinary cemeteries of monumental inscriptions to humans upon which details of a departed dog are also etched.

At Edinburgh Castle there is a rare example of a dog cemetery in which dogs belonging to the military, including mascots, have been buried since the Victorian period. Another pet cemetery was created in Hyde Park by the keeper of the Victoria Gate Lodge on the Bayswater Road, Mr Winbridge, in 1881. By 1903, when it closed, it had over 300 graves. Here, many of the people who had walked their dogs in the park laid them to rest. Uniform grey headstones with lead lettering record the dogs' names, the date of death and some very affectionate messages, such as this one: 'My Ruby Heart died Sept 14th 1897. For Seven Years We Were Such Friends.' Many of the pet owners were local to the area – wealthy people like Mr and Mrs J. Lewis Barned, whose Maltese terrier Cherry was the first to be buried there, and who lived near to the lodge at 10 Cambridge Square. Since the stones themselves do not record who the dogs' owners were, you will need to consult the Royal Parks Archive for more detail. For more information contact info@theroyalparksguild.org.

Epitaphs to dogs on gravestones and memorials could be every bit as romantic as those to humans. The most famous is probably that at Newstead Abbey, which is addressed to Boatswain, the dog of the poet Lord Byron. It reads: 'Near this spot are deposited the remains of one who possessed beauty without vanity, strength without insolence, courage without ferocity, and all the virtues of man without his vices. This praise, which would be unmeaning flattery if inscribed over human ashes, is but just tribute to Boatswain, a Dog who was born in Newfoundland 1803 and who died at Newstead Nov 18th, 1808.'

OBITUARIES

In 1850 a great celebrity of the nineteenth century, George Wombwell (b. 1776), died, and his obituary was published in *The Times* (see www.thetimes.co.uk/tto/archive). Wombwell's career as a menagerist showing snakes, tigers elephants, zebras, pumas and polar bears around Britain obviously meant that he left many animals behind him when he died, but particular mention is made of his dog – a beautiful pointer bitch – who had apparently suckled some of his lion cubs. One of Wombwell's claim to fame was that he had 'cured' Prince Albert's harrier hounds of a terrible illness (that had claimed the lives of several) by suggesting that their water was contaminated and insisting that it be changed. Wombwell is obviously a special case, but from the late nineteenth century the local newspaper obituaries of even quite ordinary people often made mention of the dogs that survived their owners. Check out newspaper records at www.britishnewspaperarchive.co.uk or www.findmypast.co.uk.

DIARIES, LETTERS, BIBLES

The births and deaths of cats and dogs are often mentioned as significant family events in diaries, letters and other personal papers. Some pets' names (and their dates of birth and death) have been found recorded alongside those of their human family in Bibles. A mid-twentieth-century family Bible belonging to the Woods family, for example, includes three unusual entries, evidently recording the death of pets: 'Tiddlewinks, May 1st 1944; Dear Pal, July 1949 at rest; Muss Muss, – another faithful Pal at rest Autumn 1955.'

FAMILY STORIES

Correctly or not, people frequently claim a role for dogs and cats when recounting family anecdotes, and often suggest that canine companions of the past mirrored the characters of their owners. Likewise, dogs appear to have played a significant part in the biographies of most of our well-known forebears. In 1837, for instance, Florence Nightingale's first patient was a sheepdog, Cap, who lived near her parents' home in Matlock and whom she saved from being destroyed after its leg was damaged by cruel children throwing stones. Keeper, the dog of the reclusive writer Emily Brontë, is said to have provided comfort for her grieving family after her untimely death. And Queen Victoria's collie dog Sharp (1866–79) apparently helped her recover from the death of Prince Albert, though he was a fierce, melancholy animal and apparently took to nobody but the queen and her ghillie, John Brown.

DOG NAMES

If you are lucky enough to come across the name of a family dog in records of one sort or another, it might be worthwhile speculating about why it acquired that particular name. The Billys, Chips and Bobbits that turn up frequently might not be of much interest, but sometimes a name was chosen because it reflected some aspect of its owner's life or experience. For example, a terrier owned by George Wombwell (mentioned above) in 1832 was unusually named Jewess, something that has led to speculation

Beauty, the dog of the magician The Great Lafayette, appears on the 1911 census as his 'daughter', and is described as being of 'independent means'. (www.thegenealogist.co.uk)

that either Wombwell himself was Jewish or that he named his pet after the people of the East End of London, where his animal 'emporium' had been located. Alfred Lord Tennyson's dog, with whom he was frequently pictured and who even appears in a famous sculpture alongside him, was named Karenina, presumably after Tolstoy's novel *Anna Karenina* (published in English in 1877). She was, after all, a Siberian wolfhound, and her literary name was very apt for her owner, the Poet Laureate.

FIND OUT MORE

Gary E. Eichorn. and Scott B. Jones, *The Dog Album: Studio Portraits of Dogs and Their People*, Stewart, Tabori and Chang, 2000.

Sheila Keenan, *Animals in the House: A History of Pets and People*, Scholastic, 1997.

William Secord, *Dog Painting: The European Breeds*, Antique Collectors' Club, 2000.

Madeline Swann and Celia Haddon, *A Curious History of Cats*, Little Books, 2005.

www.battersea.org.uk/about_us/our_history – history of Battersea Dogs Home.

www.countrysportsandcountrylife.com/sections/pedigree_dog/history_of_dog/history.htm – timeline of dates at which different breeds of dog were introduced into Britain.

www.dogbreeds.net – looks at the history of dog breeding.

www.nationalcatclub.co.uk – National Cat Club.

www.messybeast.com/history/history.htm – historical photographs of dogs and other animals.

www.thekennelclub.org – the Kennel Club, which has extensive archive and library material.

INDEX

Lightning Source UK Ltd.
Milton Keynes UK
UKOW05f1527060214

225999UK00001BB/63/P